D0862584

PUBLIC HEALTH LAW

IN A NUTSHELL®

by

JAMES G. HODGE, JR.
Associate Dean and Lincoln Professor
of Health Law and Ethics
Sandra Day O'Connor College of Law
Arizona State University

Mat #41483157

Nutshell Series, In a Nutshell and the Nutshell Logo are trademarks registered in the U.S. Patent and Trademark Office.

© 2014 LEG, Inc. d/b/a West Academic
      444 Cedar Street, Suite 700
      St. Paul, MN 55101
      1-877-888-1330

West, West Academic Publishing, and West Academic are trademarks of West Publishing Corporation, used under license.

Printed in the United States of America

ISBN: 978–0–314–28884–4

PREFACE / INTRODUCTION

The study or practice of public health law is challenging due largely to the breadth of the field. As defined in more detail in Chapter 1, public health law includes all laws that: (1) are primarily designed to assure the conditions for people to be healthy, or (2) hinder the efforts of public or private sectors to protect, promote, or preserve community health through structural- or rights-based limits.

The reach of public health law extends to traditional areas relating to the prevention and control of communicable diseases (e.g., HIV/AIDS), chronic conditions (e.g., heart disease), injuries (e.g., gunshot wounds), and other health threats (e.g., food-borne illnesses). Related to these traditional objectives are legal issues arising from the use of identifiable information for public health surveillance, regulation of property to abate nuisances, inspection of commercial establishments to detect public health risks, and limitations on the dissemination of commercial or other messages that negatively impact community health.

Under even broader conceptions, public health law envelops any legal efforts that address negative effects on human health. These may include various measures to target the underlying causes of poor health outcomes, such as lack of access to health services; socio-economic, racial, ethnic, or other disparities in the distribution of services;

homelessness or housing limitations; insufficient food or sustenance; and environmental factors, such as air or water pollution, or global climate change.

Though comprehensive in its scope, public health law has limits for the purposes of this text. To concentrate on core aspects of public health law (and also avoid duplication of material in other NUTSHELL series texts, notably ADMINISTRATIVE LAW, BIOETHICS & LAW, CONSTITUTIONAL LAW, DISABILITY LAW, ENVIRONMENTAL LAW, HEALTH CARE LAW & ETHICS, and MENTAL HEALTH LAW), this text does not include significant coverage of several legal issues even though they directly or tangentially affect the public's health. These include laws concerning access and delivery of health care services; national health care reform; disability law; environmental protection (except as related to environmental health); mental health law; and the licensure or regulation of public health or healthcare workers and entities.

A. Sources of Public Health Law

Primary sources of U.S. public health law are diverse. Given the heavy role of government in protecting the public's health, constitutional issues often arise (*see* the U.S. Constitution Bill of Rights and 14th Amendment, restated hereafter, for reference throughout the text). One of the central themes of the field is the consummate need to balance public and private interests in effectuating public health objectives and programs. Federal, tribal, state, and local lawmakers are responsible for public health statutes or other legislative enactments. Some of these legislative efforts are based on model public health acts or provisions produced via academic or other entities. Legislatures also empower public health and other executive branch agencies to create and enforce regulatory or administrative laws or issue executive orders to advance public health goals.

Courts at all levels of government contribute to the breadth and limits of public health powers through pivotal decisions on constitutional or other challenges. Collectively these cases constitute what is known as the "common law." Finally, public health law includes "soft law" examples, such as memoranda of understanding, departmental policies, letters of clarification, or other initiatives. Courts or others may assign some weight to these sources in assessing public health issues.

B. Teaching & Practicing Public Health Law

Not long ago, core courses in public health law were taught in only a handful of largely graduate-level institutions. Few practitioners nationally identified themselves as "public health lawyers." In the past 2 decades, however, public health law has emerged as a distinct field of practice and a formal course of academic study. Thousands of practitioners working in public and private sector positions have received comprehensive or select training in public health legal topics. Hundreds of core courses in public health law are taught annually in lecture, seminar, and clinical formats across the country.

Based on my 2012 survey of public health law academics, virtually all accredited schools of public health, over one-third of American Bar Association (ABA)-accredited law schools, multiple schools of medicine, and even some undergraduate institutions routinely offer core classes in public health law (often coupled with principles of ethics or policy). In addition to these core classes, many undergraduate and graduate schools offer courses in health law, bioethics, or other areas that touch prominently on public health law topics. James G. Hodge, Jr., *A Modern Survey on Teaching Public Health Law in the U.S.*, 40 J.L. MED. & ETHICS 1034 (2013).

Students across the country may find this NUTSHELL valuable as a complement to existing texts used in these courses. These texts include:

- LAWRENCE O. GOSTIN, PUBLIC HEALTH LAW AND ETHICS: A READER (2d ed. 2010) (used in my own course);

- LAW IN PUBLIC HEALTH PRACTICE (Richard A. Goodman et al. eds., 2d ed. 2007); and

- KENNETH R. WING ET AL., PUBLIC HEALTH LAW (2007), among others.

Major topics in this NUTSHELL include many of the issues addressed in these texts and courses, although under varied organizational patterns or levels of coverage. For example, while Professor Gostin disperses emergency legal preparedness issues throughout his READER, these issues are combined in the final chapter of the NUTSHELL. Review of this text's Table of Contents or the Index facilitates a quick comparison and examination of relevant passages based on study assignments or interest areas.

For public health or legal practitioners seeking a solid introduction or enhanced understanding of the field of public health law outside formal coursework, this text provides a helpful tool for "self-study," as well as a practical guide on core topics in a condensed format. Some of the practice guidance for this text stems from ongoing efforts of the Network for Public Health Law to help public health officials and their legal counsel (among many others) through specific guidance on legal issues they experience in their practice.

C. Acknowledgments

Many thanks to outstanding colleagues at institutions and locations across the country who provided their input, guidance, research, or reviews for this text. They include (in alphabetical order): Christina Arregoces, Leila F. Barraza, J.D., M.P.H., Jennifer Bernstein, J.D., M.P.H., Scott Burris, J.D., Veda Collmer, J.D., Alicia Corbett, J.D., Brooke Courtney, J.D., M.P.H., Corey Davis, J.D., M.P.H., Lance A. Gable, J.D., M.P.H., Richard A. Goodman, M.D., J.D., M.P.H., Monica Hammer, J.D., Kathleen Hoke, J.D., Peter D. Jacobson, J.D., M.P.H., Ira Kaufman, M.S., Nancy Kaufman, R.N., M.S., Stacie Kershner, J.D., Chase Millea, Rose Meltzer, Daniel G. Orenstein, J.D., Wendy E. Parmet, J.D., Tia Powell, M.D., Sonja Quinones, Clifford M. Rees, J.D., Lainie Rutkow, J.D., M.P.H., Ph.D., Debbie Snow, J.D., Stephen P. Teret, J.D., M.P.H., Jon S.

Vernick, J.D., M.P.H., Kim Weidenaar, J.D., and Lexi White.

Special thanks to Kellie Nelson and Susan Russo, both J.D. candidates at the Sandra Day O'Connor College of Law, whose contributions were indispensable to the production of the text.

Finally, I dedicate this text to Andrea, Maria, Avery, and Collin for their support and patience with its preparation and publication. Thank you.

JAMES G. HODGE, JR., J.D., LL.M.

The U.S. Constitution
Bill of Rights & 14th Amendment

Amendment I. Congress shall make no law respecting an establishment of religion, or prohibiting the free exercise thereof; or abridging the freedom of speech, or of the press; or the right of the people peaceably to assemble, and to petition the Government for a redress of grievances.

Amendment II. A well regulated Militia, being necessary to the security of a free State, the right of the people to keep and bear Arms, shall not be infringed.

Amendment III. No Soldier shall, in time of peace be quartered in any house, without the consent of the Owner, nor in time of war, but in a manner to be prescribed by law.

Amendment IV. The right of the people to be secure in their persons, houses, papers, and effects, against unreasonable searches and seizures, shall not be violated, and no Warrants shall issue, but upon probable cause, supported by Oath or affirmation, and particularly describing the place to be searched, and the persons or things to be seized.

Amendment V. No person shall be held to answer for a capital, or otherwise infamous crime, unless on a presentment or indictment of a Grand Jury, except in cases arising in the land or naval forces, or in the Militia, when in actual service in time of War or public danger; nor shall any person be subject for the same offence to be twice put in jeopardy of life or limb; nor shall be compelled in any criminal case to be a witness against himself, nor be deprived of life, liberty, or property, without due process of law; nor shall private property be taken for public use, without just compensation.

Amendment VI. In all criminal prosecutions, the accused shall enjoy the right to a speedy and public trial, by an impartial jury of the State and district wherein the crime shall have been committed, which district shall have been previously ascertained by law, and to be informed of the nature and cause of the accusation; to be confronted with the witnesses against him; to have compulsory process for obtaining witnesses in his favor, and to have the Assistance of Counsel for his defence.

Amendment VII. In Suits at common law, where the value in controversy shall exceed twenty dollars, the right of trial by jury shall be preserved, and no fact tried by a jury, shall be otherwise re-examined in any Court of the United States, than according to the rules of the common law.

Amendment VIII. Excessive bail shall not be required, nor excessive fines imposed, nor cruel and unusual punishments inflicted.

Amendment IX. The enumeration in the Constitution, of certain rights, shall not be construed to deny or disparage others retained by the people.

Amendment X. The powers not delegated to the United States by the Constitution, nor prohibited by it to the States, are reserved to the States respectively, or to the people.

Amendment XIV. Section 1. All persons born or naturalized in the United States, and subject to the jurisdiction thereof, are citizens of the United States and of the State wherein they reside. No State shall make or enforce any law which shall abridge the privileges or immunities of citizens of the United States; nor shall any State deprive any person of life, liberty, or property, without due process of law; nor deny to any person within its jurisdiction the equal protection of the laws.

Section 2. Representatives shall be apportioned among the several States according to their respective numbers, counting the whole number of persons in each State, excluding Indians not taxed. But when the right to vote at any election for the choice of electors for President and Vice-President of the United States, Representatives in Congress, the Executive and Judicial officers of a State, or the members of the Legislature thereof, is denied to any of the male inhabitants of such State, being twenty-one years of age, and citizens of the United States, or in any way abridged, except for participation in rebellion, or other crime, the basis of representation therein shall be reduced in the proportion which the number of such male citizens shall bear to the whole number of male citizens twenty-one years of age in such State.

Section 3. No person shall be a Senator or Representative in Congress, or elector of President and Vice-President, or hold any office, civil or military, under the United States, or under any State, who, having previously taken an oath, as a member of Congress, or as an officer of the United States, or as a member of any State legislature, or as an executive or judicial officer of any State, to support the Constitution of the United States, shall have engaged in insurrection or rebellion against the same, or given aid or comfort to the enemies thereof. But Congress may by a vote of two-thirds of each House, remove such disability.

Section 4. The validity of the public debt of the United States, authorized by law, including debts incurred for payment of pensions and bounties for services in suppressing insurrection or rebellion, shall not be questioned. But neither the United States nor any State shall assume or pay any debt or obligation incurred in aid of insurrection or rebellion against the United States, or any claim for the loss or emancipation of any slave; but all such debts, obligations and claims shall be held illegal and void.

Section 5. The Congress shall have the power to enforce, by appropriate legislation, the provisions of this article.

OUTLINE

PART 1. CORE STRUCTURE & BASES OF PUBLIC HEALTH LAW

PART 3. LAW & THE PROMOTION OF THE PUBLIC'S HEALTH

Chapter 7. Public Health Information Management, Privacy & Security

TABLE OF CASES

References are to Pages

GLOSSARY OF ACRONYMS

The following acronyms are used throughout the text:

ABA—American Bar Association

ABLA—Alcoholic Beverage Labeling Act

ACA—Patient Protection & Affordable Care Act

ACIP—Advisory Committee on Immunization Practices

ADA—Americans with Disabilities Act

AMA—American Medical Association

BLS—Bureau of Labor Statistics

BPA—Bisphenol A

CBRN—Chemical, biological, radiologic, nuclear

CDC—Centers for Disease Control & Prevention

CMS—Centers for Medicare & Medicaid Services

COPD—Chronic Obstructive Pulmonary Disease

CPSA—Consumer Product Safety Act

CPSC—Consumer Product Safety Commission

CRA—Civil Rights Act

CSTE—Council of State & Territorial Epidemiologists

DHHS—Department of Health & Human Services

DHS—Department of Homeland Security

DOT—Directly-observed Therapy

DUI—Driving Under the Influence

EEOC—Equal Employment Opportunity Commission

EHR—Electronic Health Record

EMAC—Emergency Management Assistance Compact

EMTALA—Emergency Medical Treatment & Labor Act

EPA—Environmental Protection Agency

EPT—Expedited Partner Therapy

EUA—Emergency Use Authorization

FDA—Food & Drug Administration

FERPA—Family Educational Rights & Privacy Act

FOIA—Freedom of Information Act

FSPTCA—Family Smoking Prevention & Tobacco Control Act

FTC—Federal Trade Commission

GINA—Genetic Information Nondiscrimination Act

HAI—Health-care Associated Infection

HCW—Health Care Worker

HIA—Health Impact Assessment

HiAP—Health in all Policies

HIE—Health Information Exchange

HIPAA—Health Insurance Portability & Accountability Act

HIV/AIDS—Human Immunodeficiency Virus/Acquired Immunodeficiency Disease Syndrome

HPV—Human Papillomavirus

IOM—Institute of Medicine

IRB—Institutional Review Board

JAMA—Journal of the American Medical Association

MDR—Multi-drug Resistant

MMWR—Morbidity & Mortality Weekly Reporter

MRSA—Methicillin-resistant Staphylococcus Aureus

MSEHPA—Model State Emergency Health Powers Act

MSPHPA—Model State Public Health Privacy Act

NDMS—National Disaster Medical System

NHLBI—National Heart, Lung & Blood Institute

NHTSA—National Highway Traffic Safety Administration

NINDS—National Institute of Neurological Disorders & Stroke

NLEA—Nutritional Labeling & Education Act

OHRP—Office for Human Research Protections

OSHA—Occupational Safety & Health Administration

PAHPA—Pandemic & All-Hazards Preparedness Act

PAHPRA—Pandemic & All-Hazards Preparedness Reauthorization Act

PCRS—Partner Counseling & Referral Service

PHA—Public Health Authority

PHE—Public Health Emergency

PHI—Protected Health Information

PHLR—Public Health Law Research

PHSA—Public Health Service Act

PI—Principal Investigator

PLCAA—Protection of Lawful Commerce in Arms Act

PREP—Public Readiness & Emergency Preparedness

PTSD—Post-traumatic Stress Disorder

SNS—Strategic National Stockpile

SSB—Sugar Sweetened Beverage

STD—Sexually Transmitted Disease

STI—Sexually Transmitted Infection

TB—Tuberculosis

TFAH—Trust for America's Health

USDA—U.S. Department of Agriculture

USPSTF—U.S. Preventative Services Task Force

WHO—World Health Organization

XDR—Extreme Drug Resistant

PUBLIC HEALTH LAW

IN A NUTSHELL

PART 1

CORE STRUCTURE & BASES OF PUBLIC HEALTH LAW

Protecting and promoting the public's health are quintessential functions of government. Public health agencies and officials at the federal, tribal, state, and local levels are each responsible (albeit in different ways) for accomplishing across societies what no person can do individually: *assuring the health of communities*. LAWRENCE O. GOSTIN, PUBLIC HEALTH LAW: POWER, DUTY, RESTRAINT 8–10 (2d ed. 2008).

Meeting this objective is not easy. It requires significant public and private sector partnerships, constant surveillance, access to accurate data, state-of-the-art research, enhanced practice methods, effective education and training, ethical guidance, respect for cultural sensitivities, and sufficient financing. It also requires the law.

Law is pivotal to nearly every public or private effort to advance the public's health. Understanding the central role of law related to the public's health begins with an assessment of its core structure and bases. Chapter 1 examines prior and contemporary conceptions of public health law. Following the introduction of a modern definition of public health law, the source and scope of these laws at each level of government are explored in Chapter 2. This includes a brief overview of the structural foundations of public health law, namely constitutional principles of separation of powers, preemption, and federalism.

Consistent with a vision of public health law that balances communal and individual interests, Chapter 3 lays out primary rights-based limitations (e.g., due process, equal protection, freedom of speech) on the powers of government to protect the public's health. For additional reference, see also the U.S. Constitution Bill of Rights and 14th Amendment after the Preface/Introduction. Together with the structural principles noted in Chapter 2, these constitutional norms are revisited often throughout Parts 2 and 3.

CHAPTER 1

THE FIELD OF PUBLIC HEALTH LAW

Public health law has evolved as threats to community health have changed along with public and private approaches to address them. Just a century ago, outbreaks of infectious diseases like smallpox, polio, yellow fever, and malaria arose commonly in many localities. HANS ZINSSER, RATS, LICE AND HISTORY: A CHRONICLE OF PESTILENCE AND PLAGUES (1963). Today, natural occurrences of smallpox are globally eradicated. Other communicable conditions are controlled and largely forgotten in the U.S., though they continue to plague populations in developing countries. GEORGE ROSEN, A HISTORY OF PUBLIC HEALTH (1993). Public health challenges in the U.S. have shifted to conditions such as HIV/AIDS, cancers and other chronic illnesses, obesity, injuries, and environmental threats. The future of public health invariably entails new risks that are currently unknown or outside the public's view.

A. PUBLIC HEALTH LAW: THEN & NOW

Though once centered largely on the control of infectious diseases and implementation of sanitary practices, FITZHUGH MULLAN, PLAGUES AND POLITICS: THE STORY OF THE U.S. PUBLIC HEALTH SERVICE 58 (1989), what it means to protect the public's health is changing. In 1988, the Institute of

Medicine (IOM) set forth a modern view of public health as ". . . what we, as a society, do collectively to assure the conditions for people to be healthy." IOM, THE FUTURE OF PUBLIC HEALTH 19 (1988). This definition reflects a considerable expansion of the mission and objectives of public health. Nearly any public or private sector intervention that directly or indirectly affects communal health is within the gambit of modern public health practice, including environmental hazards, injury prevention, occupational safety, and housing. These interventions interplay with individual efforts to make healthy choices within a society committed to abating risks to the community's health.

The value of this broader vision for public health in the modern era is undeniable. It has contributed to a more sophisticated and sweeping approach on how to engineer improved public health outcomes, distribute health resources equitably, eliminate health disparities, and counter negative impacts on population health. For example, public health advocates have promoted the concept of "health in all policies" (HiAP) to encourage greater attention to health outcomes related to specific public or private decisions (e.g., the placement, design, and construction of modern housing). Since health is fundamental to all economic sectors, policies that affect the social determinants of health (including schools, zoning, food, transportation, and workplaces) should be formulated in consideration of their potential positive and negative health impacts. IOM, FOR THE PUBLIC'S HEALTH:

REVITALIZING LAW AND POLICY TO MEET NEW CHALLENGES (2011).

In furtherance of this goal, governmental and private actors have developed innovative health impact assessments (HIAs) to better measure the public health ramifications of policies prior to their implementation. NAT'L ACADS., IMPROVING HEALTH IN THE U.S.: THE ROLE OF HIA (2011); JAMES G. HODGE, JR. ET AL., LEGAL REVIEW CONCERNING THE USE OF HIAS IN NON-HEALTH SECTORS (2012).

Conversely, some critics suggest an expansive view of the field has diluted what it means to protect the public's health. By spreading thin available resources to address sometimes tangential public health threats, some essential functions of public health are diminished or ignored. In an era in which public health agencies at all levels of government face chronic funding shortages, an expansive mission for public health may be beyond reach. Kyle Kinner & Cindy Pellegrini, *Expenditures for Public Health: Assessing Historical and Prospective Trends,* 99 AM. J. PUB. HEALTH 1780 (2009).

B. DEFINING PUBLIC HEALTH LAW

Just as the practice of public health is not static, neither is public health law; its scope and range have expanded over many years. Historic conceptions of public health law focused largely on public health powers related to communicable disease control and sanitation. In 1926, Yale University lecturer and World War II veteran

James Tobey set forth one of the earliest definitions of public health law: "Public health law is that branch of jurisprudence which [applies] common and statutory law to the principles of hygiene and sanitary science." JAMES A. TOBEY, PUBLIC HEALTH LAW: A MANUAL OF LAW FOR SANITARIANS 6–7 (1926). Tobey and other practitioners of this era mostly examined state and local laws authorizing traditional public health powers of vaccination, isolation, quarantine, testing, screening, treatment, inspection of commercial and residential premises, and abatement of unsanitary conditions or other health nuisances.

As the practice of public health shifted increasingly over the next several decades beyond infectious conditions, modern assessments of public health law emerged. In the 1st edition of his PUBLIC HEALTH LAW MANUAL in 1965, Columbia Law Professor Frank Grad reflected a broader view of public health law as including "provisions [that] have some considerable relationship to the maintenance of health and the prevention of disease."

No longer bound to historic notions of public health functions and core responsibilities, public health law continued to develop as a distinct field. In the 2nd edition of his MANUAL in 1990, Professor Grad took note: "[Public health law] seek[s] to enhance public health not only by prohibiting harmful activities or conditions but also by providing preventive and rehabilitative services to advance the health of the people . . . ." FRANK P.

GRAD, THE PUBLIC HEALTH LAW MANUAL 9 (2d ed. 1990).

The most influential contemporary definition of public health law stems from the work of Professor Lawrence Gostin at Georgetown University Law Center. In a series of articles and later his seminal texts on public health law, Professor Gostin lays out a modern conception of the field based on IOM's expansive view of public health:

Public health law [is] the study of the legal powers and duties of the state, in collaboration with its partners (e.g., health care, business, the community, the media, and academe), to ensure the conditions for people to be healthy, and of the limitations on the power of the state to constrain the autonomy, privacy, liberty, proprietary, and other legally protected interests of individuals.

LAWRENCE O. GOSTIN, PUBLIC HEALTH LAW: POWER, DUTY, RESTRAINT 4 (2d ed. 2008).

Professor Gostin's definition refers for the first time to the compelling balance at work in public health law between the powers of government to act "to ensure the conditions to be healthy" and the constraints on these powers to protect individual rights. Under this view, neither public health powers nor individual freedoms are absolute. Rather, they are consistently at play in determining the breadth and limit of the role of law in the interests of communal health. Professor Wendy Parmet at Northeastern School of Law recognizes this same dynamic when she notes "[p]ublic health law ... focuses on the authority of government agencies charged with protecting public health as well as the rights of individuals subject to such regulations." WENDY E. PARMET, POPULATIONS, PUBLIC HEALTH, AND THE LAW 212–13 (2009).

These sophisticated themes not only raised the scholarly level of study of public health law, they also clarified its practice. Public health law is not solely about governments' inherent powers nor individuals' fundamental rights. It is about how these respective components merge to generate meaningful and defensible legal interventions to advance the population's health.

Based on these varied approaches, for the purposes of this text, I define *public health law* as those laws (e.g., constitutional, statutory, regulatory, judicial), legal processes, or policies at every level of government (e.g., federal, tribal, state, local) that:

(1)   are *primarily* designed to assure the conditions for people to be healthy; or

(2)   concern structural or rights-based limitations on the powers of government to act in the interests of communal health.

At the epicenter of this and other modern definitions of public health law is the dynamic interplay of legal powers and restraints central to the accomplishment of public health objectives through law. Like Professor Gostin, I incorporate IOM's conception of assuring conditions for people to be healthy. This view intimates a broad and active role for law beyond mere control of communicable diseases and improvement of sanitation. The extension of law in diverse areas like education, transportation, and housing to protect and promote health among populations is core to the modern field.

My definition also acknowledges significant limitations on the role of law. While laws can obligate public and private sectors to act in the interests of the public's health, they simultaneously curtail these powers. Unlike Professor Gostin's definition, which concentrates on rights-based limitations, my definition specifically recognizes rights-based *and* structural limitations on the public health powers of government. Discussed in more detail in Chapter 2, structural limits include principles of separation of powers (delineating responsibilities among the 3 branches of government) and federalism (distinguishing between federal and state governmental authorities). Rights-based limits embedded in constitutional norms and other laws include individual rights to free expression, freedom of religion, bodily integrity, privacy, equal protection, and due process.

Though still vast, public health law is corralled by my specification that any such law be ***primarily*** designed to assure healthy conditions. This qualification is meant to help rein in the field by excluding from its study those laws that may have only tertiary or unintended effects on the public's health. As noted in the Preface, many laws have some effect on communal health; not all of them fall squarely within the field of public health law for the purposes of its assessment and practice.

By way of an illustration, consider two types of local zoning laws. In one case, a city enacts a zoning ordinance directly to advance the public's health by limiting the numbers or locations of fast food restaurants near elementary or secondary schools. This type of modern zoning law attempts to further the public's health by limiting kids' access to fast food to lower childhood obesity, a major national objective. As such, it fits neatly within the field. Like many public health laws, it also raises some controversy as to whether government can control private market choices to locate lawful businesses based solely on negating some potential impacts on childrens' health (*see* Chapter 9).

Contrast this first example with a second local zoning law requiring private planners to limit the size and placement of commercial signage in suburban areas. The primary objective of the law is to preserve or enhance the natural beauty of the area. A secondary effect of the law is to limit the commercial visibility of specific businesses (e.g., tobacco shops and liquor stores), leading some consumers to access these businesses less often or not at all. Ultimately, decreasing consumer access to tobacco and alcohol may have beneficial public health benefits, but this type of zoning law falls outside the scope of public health law via my proffered definition because its primary purpose is not to assure the conditions for people to be healthy.

For additional discussion of the potential public health uses of zoning regarding the built environment, see Chapter 9.

Distinguishing between these zoning laws may seem non-purposeful when both could positively impact the public's health. Some public health practitioners may strongly advocate for the implementation of aesthetic zoning laws largely because of their community health benefits regardless of whether city council members approve, or even know about, the public health implications. Yet, broadening the principal study of public health law to any statute, regulation, or other law having any tangential effect on the health of communities extends the field well beyond the scope of this text.

C. BUILDING EVIDENCE FOR PUBLIC HEALTH LAW

One of the dominant themes emanating from modern conceptions of the field is how law is an affirmative tool for public health improvements. What this means is that law (like other tools available to public health practitioners such as surveillance, epidemiologic investigations, or educational campaigns) can be used effectively to accomplish communal health goals.

In some cases, law is the principal means to achieve a public health outcome. For years after the advent of effective and safe vaccines for childhood diseases, thousands of children nationally continued to develop preventable conditions. In response, many state legislatures enacted school vaccination laws (conditioning attendance at school upon proof of vaccination for specified conditions) in the early 1900s. As a direct result, childhood vaccination rates climbed and related morbidity and mortality plummeted, demonstrating the efficacy of school vaccination laws. *See, e.g.,* James G. Hodge, Jr. & Lawrence O. Gostin, *School Vaccination Requirements: Historical, Social, and Legal Perspectives*, 90 KY. L.J. 831 (2002). School (and day-care) vaccination laws continue to be a core component of child and adolescent health policy (discussed initially in Chapter 3 and later in Chapter 4).

While the efficacy of vaccination laws is firmly established, many other public health laws lack a sufficient nexus with public health improvements. Reflecting a patchwork approach, many tribal, state, and local jurisdictions have passed or implemented public health laws over decades that are merely thought to be functional. Though well-intended, these laws may be supported more so by political guesswork or anecdotal cases than efficacy. Initially, few researchers explored the effectiveness of law as a public health tool even as laws increasingly became a mode of choice to address known public health threats. Scott Burris & Evan D. Anderson, *Legal Regulation of Health-Related Behavior: A Half-Century of Public Health Law Research*, 9 ANN. REV. L. & SOC. SCI., July 16, 2013.

Believing law is an effective tool for improving public health outcomes is an insufficient basis for legal intervention. Proof of efficacy may be needed to counteract politicized arguments against the use of law to address public health threats such as obesity, tobacco advertisements, and gun-related violence. Generating greater support on the effectiveness of public health laws is the focus of a modern research initiative launched in 2009 through the Public Health Law Research (PHLR) program funded by the Robert Wood Johnson Foundation. Program leader, Professor Scott Burris, and Professor Alexander Wagenaar define "public health law research" as "the scientific study of the relation of law and legal practices to population health." ALEXANDER C. WAGENAAR & SCOTT BURRIS, PUBLIC HEALTH LAW RESEARCH: THEORY AND METHODS 4 (2013).

PHLR grantees conduct independent research and examine existing evidence on the role of law in varied public health topics. For example, researchers have generated or found evidence to support the effectiveness of laws and policies in support of:

- Fluoridating water to reduce tooth decay and improve oral health;

- Raising taxes on alcohol to reduce overall consumption;

- Requiring directed patrols to lower gun-related crime by uncovering and deterring illegal gun possession in high-risk areas;

- Mandating use of child safety seats to substantially reduce injuries to children during vehicular crashes; and

- Using drug courts focused on treatment and rehabilitation to lower recidivism among individuals convicted of drug-related offenses in lieu of more traditional punitive approaches.

D. THE ROLE OF PUBLIC HEALTH ETHICS

Acknowledging an expansive (and increasingly proven) role of law to protect the public's health may suggest that law- and policy-makers can use law at will to motivate or require choices or behaviors among individuals and groups. To be sure, law has been wielded in heavy-handed ways in the guise of promoting the community's health. Historic examples discussed later in the text include numerous instances in which state and local governments confined, vaccinated, tested, or imposed other measures on unwilling individuals without sufficient justification in the name of public health prevention and control.

The legality of public health interventions, however, cannot be divorced from their ethicality. Principles of ethics not only influence the development and enforcement of law, they often provide guidance where the law cannot. For example, public health law may allow for the confinement of persons with infectious diseases like tuberculosis (TB) when they present a threat to others. *See* SHEILA M. ROTHMAN, LIVING IN THE SHADOW OF DEATH: TB AND THE SOCIAL EXPERIENCE OF ILLNESS IN AMERICAN HISTORY (1994). An individual's liberties may be curtailed legally when that individual poses serious risks to others related to infectious diseases (*see* Chapter 4). However, ethical norms limit the appropriate use of these legal authorities to those rare cases where individuals refuse either to voluntarily participate in treatment programs or defuse the risks of transmitting TB to others. Increasingly, modern TB control laws reflect this ethic of voluntarism to respect individual autonomy to the fullest extent possible even when others' health is at some slight risk.

The contributions of ethics in public health practice and policy are undeniable. As its own distinct field, public health ethics seeks to balance individual rights with the community's health needs. *See, e.g.,* PUB. HEALTH LEADERSHIP SOC'Y, PRINCIPLES OF THE ETHICAL PRACTICE OF PUBLIC HEALTH (2002) (setting forth 12 core principles). Built on the utilitarian goal of achieving the greatest health outcomes for the largest numbers possible, public health ethics reflect norms from other frameworks (such as the principles of autonomy, beneficence, non-malificence, and justice at the heart of bioethics), but they are in fact distinct.

Core principles of public health ethics center on the inherent moral responsibilities of providing for the public's health through government and the private sector. James C. Thomas et al., *A Code of Ethics for Public Health*, 92 AM. J. PUB. HEALTH 1057 (2002). They pertain not merely to those who practice public health sciences or deliver services (many of whom may also adhere to ethics codes for their respective professions), but also to how public health initiatives are applied. Public health actors must assure their interventions are effective, necessary, proportional, and transparent. James Childress et al., *Public Health Ethics: Mapping the Terrain*, 30 J.L. MED. & ETHICS 170 (2002). Consistent with modern social justice theory, limited resources must be fairly allocated and communal burdens adequately shared. MADISON POWERS & RUTH FADEN, SOCIAL JUSTICE: THE MORAL FOUNDATIONS OF PUBLIC HEALTH AND HEALTH POLICY (2006).

Making decisions consistent with applied principles of public health ethics can be complicated, especially if government acts in paternal ways to the detriment of individual choice. Though legally sound and often democratically-driven, programmatic decisions that dictate the terms in which autonomous persons must behave or adhere to specific protocols are ethically suspect. Thus, while government can require children to be vaccinated as a condition of school attendance, legally mandating that adults (e.g., emergency room nurses) be vaccinated is ethically challenging. Many health professionals view a government's or hospital's issuance of vaccine mandates as coercive even if the mandates reflect a duty among providers to protect patient safety and are empirically shown to reduce patient harms. *See* Richard K. Zimmerman et al., *Hospital Policies, State Laws, and Healthcare Worker Influenza Rates*, 34

INFECTION CONTROL & HOSP. EPIDEMIOLOGY 854 (2013); Alexandra M. Stewart et al., *Mandatory Vaccination of Health-Care Personnel: Good Policy, Law, and Outcomes*, 53 JURIMETRICS J. 431 (2013). Other measures, such as laws mandating seatbelt use in vehicles or helmets when operating motorcycles or bicycles, may be viewed as overly paternalistic.

An alternative view is advanced by Richard Thaler and Cass Sunstein through their concept of *libertarian paternalism*. They posit how institutions can "self-consciously [attempt] to move people in directions that will make their lives better," without necessarily curbing individual choice. RICHARD H. THALER & CASS R. SUNSTEIN, NUDGE: IMPROVING DECISIONS ABOUT HEALTH, WEALTH, AND HAPPINESS 6 (2009). Thus, while the public retains its freedom of choice consistent with libertarianism, government is empowered to influence personal choices. Instead of government making people purchase broccoli (which was famously argued in the health care reform debates in 2011–2012), it might consider requiring the placement of healthier foods at eye level in stores to encourage their consumption. *Id.*

Professor Nancy Kass at the Johns Hopkins Bloomberg School of Public Health lays out a series of ethical steps to consider before implementation of any public health program or intervention:

- Identify goals that aid in decreasing morbidity or mortality;

- Determine whether data exist to indicate that tactics will be effective;

- Consider potential burdens, particularly risks to privacy, liberty, and justice;

- See whether alternatives would mitigate these burdens while maintaining effectiveness;

- Distribute benefits and burdens fairly based on data rather than arbitrary or stereotypical reasons; and

- Analyze whether the benefits outweigh the burdens.

Nancy E. Kass, *An Ethics Framework for Public Health*, 91 AM. J. PUB. HEALTH 1776 (2001).

Despite early views that limited the role of law to traditional public health areas of infectious disease control and sanitation, the field has matured to encompass a plethora of laws and policies. The fabric of public health law ties together public health practice, science, politics, and ethics to promote community health and safety. Relying on more than historic tradition and modern guesswork, new research may reveal the efficacy of specific public health legal interventions. Law can be a tool for positive public health outcomes. Realizing its full potential, however, requires a strong understanding of the source and scope of public health laws at the federal, tribal, state, and local levels. This is the focus of Chapter 2.

CHAPTER 2

SOURCE & SCOPE OF PUBLIC HEALTH LEGAL POWERS

The source and scope of governmental powers to address communal health are core to the definition of public health law. Protecting the population's health is a fundamental responsibility of government. However, determining which level of government is empowered to implement and enforce public health laws is not always certain. Federal, tribal, state, and local governments often work together to address public health issues. Yet, sometimes they clash over who is in charge, or refuse to address public health initiatives even though they clearly have the legal power to act. The authority to act legally in the interest of the public's health hinges on the distribution of powers outlined in the U.S. Constitution.

Constitutional obligations of government to protect individuals and populations from communal health threats vary. Government's health responsibilities related to specific persons (e.g., prisoners, institutionalized persons with mental disabilities) are linked to these persons' non-autonomous status. Prisoners, for example, are wards of the state by virtue of their incarceration. Federal constitutional principles related to prohibitions against cruel and unusual punishments via the 8th Amendment necessitate the provision of basic health and public health services within correctional facilities. *Brown v. Plata*, 131 S. Ct. 1910 (2011) (medical and mental health care provided in California's prisons fell below the standard of decency required by the 8th Amendment due in part to overcrowding).

Protecting the health of other vulnerable persons or the general public, however, is not guaranteed. In most cases, government is not required to assure the health of specific individuals, much less the public. In *DeShaney v. Winnebago Cnty. Dep't of Soc. Serv.*, 489 U.S. 189 (1989), for example, the U.S. Supreme Court considered a child's claim against Wisconsin county agencies . Joshua DeShaney was mercilessly abused by his father while supposedly under the watchful eye of local child welfare services. Eventually, the child suffered permanent physical and mental injuries. Joshua and his mother sued, alleging that Wisconsin officials deprived Joshua of his liberty under the Due Process Clause of the 14th Amendment. In dismissing the claim, Chief Justice Rehnquist, writing for the majority, famously concluded that absent a "special relationship" (e.g., related to prisoners or other wards), "a State's failure to protect an individual against private violence simply does not constitute a violation of [due process]." *Id.* at 197. "Poor Joshua," lamented Justice Blackmun in his dissent. *Id.* at 213.

In 2005, the Court clarified that due process rights also did not confer a property interest sufficient to assure government action concerning a woman seeking enforcement of a restraining order issued by a local court in Colorado. *See Castle Rock v. Gonzales*, 545 U.S. 748 (2005). Based on these and related decisions, the U.S. Constitution has not been interpreted to require federal or state governments to assure communal health. Contrast this position with constitutional "right to health" clauses in multiple other countries that are interpreted to include basic public health services and duties. *See, e.g.*, Benjamin M. Meier et al., *Bridging International Law and Rights-Based Litigation: Mapping Health-Related Rights Through the Development of the Global Health and Human Rights Law Database*, 14 HEALTH & HUM. RTS.: INT'L J. 1 (2012).

A.   THE CONSTITUTIONAL FOUNTAIN OF PUBLIC HEALTH POWERS

While the Constitution does not require government to assure the conditions for people to be healthy, it does set the legal foundation for public and private health interventions.   Principles of constitutional design (1) allocate power between the federal government and the states (a.k.a. federalism); (2) divide power among the 3 branches of government (a.k.a. separation of powers), and (3) limit government power (to protect individual freedoms, discussed in Chapter 3).   In these ways, the Constitution acts like a fountain (originating the flow of power to protect the public's health) and a levee (curbing that power to protect individual interests).

1.   FEDERALISM

Among the unique facets of American democracy is the Constitutional principle of federalism. Federalism distinguishes the powers among the levels of governments. As explained below, the powers of the national government are enumerated and limited. Through the 10th Amendment, states were reserved sovereign power over "all the objects, which, in the ordinary course of affairs, concern the lives, liberties and properties of the people; and the internal order, improvement, and prosperity of the State." U.S. CONST. amend. X. These residual powers authorize states to regulate matters affecting the health, safety, and general welfare of the public and its citizens.

Though ingenious in constitutional design, federalism as applied is not always predictable. There is no bright line separating federal and state authorities. In reality, governments' respective powers have historically overlapped, especially in areas like public health. In many cases, principles of cooperative federalism render agreeable outcomes. Yet, when federal and state powers collide, the application of federalism takes on many shades and near imperceptible gradations. James G. Hodge, Jr., *The Role of New Federalism and Public Health Law*, 12 J.L. & HEALTH 309, 316 (1998).

For example, states may (a) seek to invade areas set aside for exclusive federal interventions (e.g., enacting laws which interfere with Congress' regulation of interstate commerce) or (b) fail to recognize federal supremacy or authority (e.g., attempting to impose taxes on federal goods). These latter actions were more common in the nation's early history as states tested the limits of their sovereign powers. However, modern debates about the scope of Congress' powers to increase access to health services through the Affordable Care Act (ACA) reflect similar themes. *National Fed. of Ind. Bus. v. Sebelius,* 132 S. Ct. 2566 (2012) (discussed below); *see also* PATIENT CARE AND PROFESSIONALISM (Catherine D. DeAngelis ed., 2014).

Conversely, the federal government may intrude upon traditional state duties. Historically, federal exercises which interfered with traditional state powers were politically volatile. They were struck down routinely by courts that assigned considerable weight to sovereign state police powers under the 10th Amendment. *See Hammer v. Dagenhart,* 247 U.S. 251 (1918) (federal statute prohibiting the interstate commerce of child labor products infringed on the states' power to regulate child labor hours); later overruled in *U.S. v. Darby,* 312 U.S. 100 (1941).

In theory, federal laws which moved into areas traditionally left to the states were beyond Congress' jurisdiction and therefore unconstitutional. Federal expansion during the New Deal Era (1933~1938) relaxed traditional conceptions of federalism, ushering in numerous federal interventions in public health and other areas. These include establishment of the U.S. Public Health Service in 1939 and the Centers for

Disease Control in 1946. *See* Hodge, *The Role of New Federalism*, 12 J.L. & HEALTH at 335–36. Supreme Court jurisprudence accommodated these changes in many ways. In 1941, the Court observed in *U.S. v. Darby*, 312 U.S. 100, 115 (1941), that Congress' power may be "attended by the same incidents [as the] exercise of the police power of the states." Later years saw the introduction of sweeping federal health care reforms through the Social Security Act Amendments of 1965, 42 U.S.C. § 1395 (2010), establishing Medicare and Medicaid programs.

After decades of federal expansion into the public health sphere, political and judicial actors rediscovered core principles of federalism. Collectively labeled "new federalism" by constitutional scholars in the 1990s, a series of influential decisions by the U.S. Supreme Court resulted in its:

- adoption of a strong rule against federal invasion of "core state functions;"

- presumption against application of federal statutes to state and local political processes;

- disdain for federal action that "commandeers" state governments into the service of federal regulatory purposes;

- rejection of federal claims brought by private parties against states; and

- application of a plain statement rule that Congress must ". . . make its intention . . . unmistakably clear in the language of the statute" whenever it seeks to preempt state law so as to alter the balance of federalism. *Gregory v. Ashcroft*, 501 U.S. 452, 460 (1991).

Principles of new federalism re-opened state challenges of some federal public health laws on 10th Amendment grounds. ERWIN CHEMERINSKY, CONSTITUTIONAL LAW: PRINCIPLES AND POLICIES 269–74 (4th ed. 2011). The Supreme Court's decision in *U.S. v. Lopez*, 514 U.S. 549 (1995), is illustrative. The Court held that Congress exceeded its Commerce powers by statutorily making gun possession within a local school zone a federal criminal offense. Finding that possessing a gun within a school zone did not "substantially affect" interstate commerce, the Court declared the statute unconstitutional despite the laudable, underlying public health objective of preventing gun-related violence at or near schools. *Id.* at 567.

Federalism continues to dominate political and judicial processes. In 2012, the Supreme Court opined that Congress lacked the Commerce power to require individuals to purchase health insurance (a.k.a. "individual mandate") via the ACA. Writing for the Court, Chief Justice Roberts found instead that Congress' power to tax was sufficiently broad to justify the mandate. *Sebelius,* 132 S. Ct. at 2600. As a result, ACA's fundamental requirement that individuals purchase health insurance was upheld under federal tax authority, but not through Congress' power to regulate interstate commerce, thus preserving some traditional state-based authorities.

2.   SEPARATION OF POWERS

The federal Constitution (as well as states' constitutions) separate governmental powers into 3 branches: (a) the legislative branch (with the power to create laws); (b) the executive branch (with the power to enforce laws); and (c) the judicial branch (with the power to interpret laws). Constitutional separation of governmental powers not only provides a system of checks and balances, it also helps curb the potential for government oppression.

Pursuant to the separation of powers doctrine, each branch of government has unique constitutional authority to create, enforce, or interpret public health law and policy. Federal and state legislatures largely create health policy and allocate necessary resources to effectuate it. To accomplish this goal, legislators need reliable, accurate information on public health threats and interventions to make complex decisions that are also consistent with their constituents' interests, competing claims, and constitutional limits. *See* Chapter 7 for additional discussion.

The executive branch (primarily through public health departments or agencies) enforces health policy via delegated legislative authority. Such delegations can be extensive or narrow. For example, in creating a state public health agency, a state legislature may bestow it with broad powers to protect the public's health. Later, the legislature may then direct the agency to perform specific functions (e.g., conduct an HIA related to a transportation project). In either example, public health agencies take some direction from the legislature and must act accordingly within the scope of their delegated power. Federal and state executive agencies sometimes work in tandem with lawmakers to determine the extent and course of public health policies. In other cases, conflicts can arise such as when public health agencies attempt to create and administer complex health regulations which some legislators may not agree with in principle or policy.

Provided that legislatures articulate standards for issuance and enforcement of these regulations, the Supreme Court has approved such delegations consistent with principles of separation of powers. *See Chevron, U.S.A., Inc. v. NRDC, Inc.,* 467 U.S. 837 (1984). Sometimes executive agencies exceed the bounds of their legislative delegation. In *Boreali v. Axelrod,* 71 N.Y.2d 1 (Ct. App. N.Y. 1987), for example, New York's Public Health Council promulgated a comprehensive code to govern tobacco smoking in public areas. Although the New York state legislature authorized the Council to regulate generally in the interests of the public's health, the court found the Council overstepped its authority when it attempted to regulate tobacco far outside the bounds of its legislative delegation. In 2013, a New York appellate court used the same approach taken in *Boreali* to strike down a proposed ban on large portion sizes of sugar-sweetened beverages (SSBs). *N.Y. Statewide Coal. of Hispanic Chambers of Commerce v. N.Y. Dep't of Health and Mental Hygiene*, No. 653584/12 (N.Y. App. Div. July 30, 2013); *see* Chapter 8 for additional discussion.

The judiciary is tasked with interpreting the law to resolve disputes. Courts exert substantial influence in public health law and policy. They decide whether public health statutes or regulations are constitutional, agency actions are legislatively authorized, public health officials have gathered sufficient evidence to support their interventions, and public or private actors are negligent. Deciding these types of issues is challenging.

Courts are bound by precedent (i.e., prior judicial decisions) and tend to defer to the policy decisions of state and local lawmakers under the separation of powers doctrine. As a result, judges often strive to decide cases consistent with the underlying intent of statutory or administrative laws. Still, judicial decisions on public health matters vary extensively for many reasons. Precedent extends only as far as a court's jurisdiction. Thus, while the U.S. Supreme Court's decisions on federal constitutional law have precedential value nationally, a state supreme court's decision on a matter of state law does not require another state's courts to decide a similar issue the same way.

Divergent judicial results also arise from the fact that some judges are politically elected (rather than appointed) or because of the unique facts of a particular case. Courts less familiar with public health issues or data may decide cases in reliance on different information. *See, e.g.,* N.Y. STATE PUBLIC HEALTH LEGAL MANUAL: A GUIDE FOR JUDGES, ATTORNEYS, AND PUBLIC HEALTH PROFESSIONALS (Michael Colodner ed., 2011). Courts nationally struggle to distinguish valid scientific evidence (*see Daubert v. Merrell Dow Pharmaceuticals, Inc.*, 509 U.S. 579 (1993)) from "junk science" advanced by "denialists." *See* Leila Barraza et al., *Denialism and its Adverse Effect on Public Health*, 53 JURIMETRICS J. 307 (2013). For an illustration of divergent court decisions on the constitutionality of tobacco warning labels, *see* Chapter 8.D.

B. FEDERAL PUBLIC HEALTH POWERS

In theory, the federal government has limited, defined powers. Consistent with principles of federalism, Congress draws its authority to act from specific, enumerated powers granted pursuant to Article II of the Constitution. These include the power to regulate interstate commerce, tax, and set conditions on federal spending. The aforementioned political and judicial expansion of these powers (through what is known as the doctrine of implied powers) allows the federal government considerable authority to act in the interests of public health and safety. The federal government may employ all means reasonably appropriate to achieve the objectives of its listed powers, including raising revenue for public health services and regulating private activities that endanger human health.

To preserve federal exercises of powers from intrusion or interference by state and local governments, the Supremacy Clause of the Constitution (art. VI, cl. 2) provides that federal constitutional, statutory, regulatory, and judicial laws preempt state and local laws. *See* CHEMERINSKY, CONSTITUTIONAL LAW, at 402–27. In the context of public health, federal preemption is a double-edged sword. Congressional passage of key pieces of legislation concerning vehicle safety, food policy, national security, environmental protection, transportation, and access to health services, among other areas, establish national, uniform standards essential to achieve public health objectives. Conflicting state laws are preempted. Depending on the extent of Congressional direction, state laws that provide less restrictive standards may also be preempted if meeting a lower standard defeats the purpose of federal law. *See, e.g., Shilling v. Moore*, 545 N.W.2d 442 (Neb. 1996) (to the extent the federal Health Care Quality Improvement Act affords greater protection for medical peer reviewers facing defamation actions than Nebraska's state law, Nebraska's law is preempted).

In some areas, such as environmental protection, federal law may "occupy the field" so completely as to negate any state or local regulations in the same area (even if federal law is insufficient to achieve essential public health outcomes). In this way, preemption can thwart public health legal interventions when federal law strips state or local governments of their ability to address public health issues. *See, e.g., U.S. v. City & Cnty. of Denver*, 100

F.3d 1509 (10th Cir. 1996) (Comprehensive Environmental Response, Compensation, and Liability Act preempted Denver's zoning ordinance prohibiting the maintenance of hazardous waste).

C. STATE PUBLIC HEALTH POWERS

Unlike the federal government's enumerated powers, states possess extensive authority to protect the public's health. Their public health powers derive largely from sovereign powers reserved to the states via the 10th Amendment and may extend to local governments through state delegations. The expansive and dominant role of state governments in public health is directly related to the breadth of their police and *parens patriae* powers, each of which is explained below.

1. POLICE POWERS

Often thought of as the powers of government to conduct law enforcement activities, state "police powers" are much broader in scope. They represent the state's primary source of power to promote the general welfare of society. Historically, police powers have been defined as "the inherent authority of the state to enact laws and promulgate regulations to protect, preserve and promote the health, safety, morals, and general welfare of the people." ERNST FREUND, THE POLICE POWER: PUBLIC POLICY AND CONSTITUTIONAL RIGHTS 3–4 (1904). In 2006, the Supreme Court noted how principles of federalism "allow the States great latitude under their police powers to legislate [to protect] the lives,

limbs, health, comfort, and quiet of all persons."
Gonzales v. Oregon, 546 U.S. 243, 270 (2006).

Police powers underlie most laws to prevent
morbidity and mortality across populations. They
are the source of public health powers to test,
screen, vaccinate, treat, quarantine, and isolate
individuals. They authorize as well the creation of
state and local public health agencies, empowering
them to conduct educational campaigns,
surveillance, and epidemiological investigations.
Many additional public health authorities discussed
throughout the text are supported by state police
powers. In furtherance of these powers, states may
restrict (within federal and state constitutional
limits) private interests in liberty, autonomy, and
privacy, as well as economic interests in freedom to
contract and use of property. *Allied Structural Steel
Co. v. Spannaus,* 438 U.S. 234, 241 (1978).

2.   PARENS PATRIAE POWERS

In addition to their sovereign police powers,
states also possess *parens patriae* powers.
Translated literally as the "parent of the country,"
these powers authorize state government not only to
act in the interests of the community's well-being,
but also in relation to individuals' own best
interests. LAWRENCE O. GOSTIN, PUBLIC HEALTH
LAW: POWER, DUTY, RESTRAINT 95–96 (2d ed. 2008).

Parens patriae powers are invoked in 2 major
ways. First, the state may seek legal standing in
cases supporting the community's health and
welfare (e.g., the state sues the federal government

on behalf of the state's citizens to compel specific public health goals). *See, e.g., Massachusetts v. EPA*, 549 U.S. 497 (2007) (requesting Environmental Protection Agency (EPA) to regulate emissions of greenhouse gases). Second, the state may serve as guardian of, or provide protections for, persons who may otherwise lack capacity to look after their own interests or welfare. *Parens patriae* powers in this context allow the state to step in for the benefit of minors, persons with mental disabilities, the elderly, or prisoners or other "wards" of the state to avert or correct known physical or mental harms. For example, state government may rely on its *parens patriae* powers to protect a child from mental or physical abuse or neglect (*see Santosky v. Kramer*, 455 U.S. 745 (1982)); institutionalize a person with mental instabilities who poses a risk to him- or herself (*see Mezick v. State*, 920 S.W.2d 427 (Tex. App. 1996)); or prevent harms to incapacitated older persons from their caretakers (*see Congress Care Ctr. Assoc. v. Chicago Dep't of Health*, 632 N.E.2d 266 (Ill. App. Ct. 1994)).

Use of state-based *parens patriae* powers can be controversial when constitutional rights of the individual are at stake. In *Clark v. Cohen*, 794 F.2d 79 (3d Cir. 1986), Carolyn Clark was confined at a state-run mental institution for 28 years without notice or a hearing despite her repeated requests to receive training on how to live independently. After her release, she sued. The 3rd Circuit federal Court of Appeals affirmed that Clark's involuntary confinement violated her constitutional right to liberty and procedural due process. The court noted:

"To deprive any citizen of his or her liberty upon the altruistic theory that the confinement is for humane therapeutic reasons and then fail to provide adequate treatment violates the very fundamentals of due process." *Id.* at 94 (citing *Wyatt v. Stickney*, 325 F. Supp. 781, 785 (M.D. Ala. 1971)).

D. LOCAL PUBLIC HEALTH POWERS

County, city, or other local public health officials are on the front line of public health practice. They are directly responsible for conducting public health surveillance, implementing federal and state programs, operating public health clinics, and setting public health policies for their specific populations. The performance of local (and state) public health agencies may be evaluated consistent with national accreditation standards. Kim Krisberg, *Eleven Health Departments First to Attain Public Health Accreditation*, 43 THE NATION'S HEALTH 1 (2013).

Local governments' authority to act in the interests of the public's health extends largely from broad or narrow delegations of state police powers via state constitutional, legislative, or executive means. Such delegations provide local governments with a limited realm of authority, or "home rule," over public health matters of local concern within their jurisdiction. ANTIEAU ON LOCAL GOVERNMENT LAW § 21.01 (2d ed. 2006); *see also City of Chicago v. Taylor*, 774 N.E.2d 22, 26–27 (Ill. App. Ct. 2002) (home rule is premised on the idea that local governments are best-positioned to assess their communities' needs and enact laws addressing local concerns). State legislatures may modify, clarify, preempt, or remove home rule at will, unless it is protected by state constitutions.

Exercises of local authority in the interests of public health can neither extend beyond limited jurisdictional boundaries nor conflict with or impair federal or state law. In 2001, for example, the city of Cleveland relied on its home rule powers to pass an ordinance prohibiting liquor advertising on billboards and other public signs. When an outdoor advertising firm sued to enjoin the city from enforcing the provisions, the court found that the ordinance was preempted by state law allowing alcohol advertising (and in violation of constitutional commercial speech protections, discussed in Chapter 8). *See Eller Media Co. v. City of Cleveland,* 161 F. Supp. 2d 796 (N.D. Ohio 2001).

Local governments' home rule authority may also be limited judicially. Through what is known as "Dillon's Rule," based on the holdings and scholarship of Iowa Supreme Court Justice John F. Dillon in the late 1800s, local governments are limited to those authorities expressly granted to them by state legislatures. Dillon's Rule suggests that local governments may exercise only those powers expressly granted or necessarily implied via statute, unless it is vested with broad home rule. JOHN F. DILLON, THE LAW OF MUNICIPAL CORPORATIONS 173 (2d ed. 1873).

Modern applications of Dillon's Rule are muted. For example, the Tennessee Supreme Court opined in 2001 that strict construction of the limits of local power is only appropriate when there is a complete lack of, or ambiguity in, state legislative intent. Thus, Dillon's Rule may not apply whenever a state legislature clearly grants comprehensive authority to a local government, or the locality regulates in the interests of the public's health. *Southern Constructors, Inc. v. Loudon Cnty. Bd. of Educ.*, 58 S.W.3d 706 (Tenn. 2001).

E.   TRIBAL PUBLIC HEALTH POWERS

Unlike state and local governments, tribal governments owe their legal existence to the federal government, from which many of their public health powers flow. In the mid-1800s, the federal government granted many American Indians limited set-asides of land (reservations) on which they formed sovereign tribal governments eligible for direct federal assistance. As sovereigns, tribal governments have public health powers similar to states. In practice, however, protecting the health of the tribal populations is a shared venture between federal, state, and tribal governments.

Pursuant to the Snyder Act of 1921, 25 U.S.C. § 13, Congress directly assumed responsibility for providing health care services to tribal governments. Federal assistance continues through long-term commitments for comprehensive health services administered by the Indian Health Service, part of the Department of Health and Human Services (DHHS), and the Bureau of Indian Affairs. Over many years Congress has legislatively committed resources, facilities, and personnel to provide health care benefits to American Indians through collaborative efforts. The ACA has further strengthened the federal role through long-term financial and resource commitments. Indian Health Care Improvement Act, 25 U.S.C. §§ 1601–1683 (2010).

Management and supervision of Indian public health programs and facilities are left generally to tribal governments as part of a movement toward self-governance, furthered by Congress' enactment of the Tribal Self-Governance Act of 1994, 25 U.S.C. §§ 450–458hh (2012). Federally-recognized tribes may use Indian Health Service funds for specific health programs consistent with general conditions. This flexibility allows tribal governments to target and respond to differing health needs across their populations.

———————

As discussed in this chapter, the powers of government to protect the public's health are extensive and overlapping. Inevitable conflicts between the levels (federal, tribal, state, local) and branches (legislative, executive, judicial) of governments evoke constitutional principles of federalism and separation of powers. These structural principles determine which level or branch is authorized to act in the interests of the public's health. Assessing the full constitutional limits of public health powers requires further exploration. Chapter 3 introduces how individual rights counter-balance governments' broad powers to protect the public's health, and then explains how structural and rights-based norms are interconnected through one of the seminal cases in public health law, *Jacobson v. Massachusetts*, 197 U.S. 11 (1905).

CHAPTER 3

CONSTITUTIONAL RIGHTS & THE PUBLIC'S HEALTH

In addition to creating a structural foundation for the assignment and execution of governmental public health powers, the federal Constitution limits these powers through affirmative protections of individual rights and liberties. The Bill of Rights (the first 10 amendments to the Constitution), the 14th amendment, and other constitutional provisions create a zone of individual rights that government may not invade absent justification. At the crux of public health in theory and practice is the need to balance tensions between population-based laws and individual rights.

A. FOUNDATIONS OF RIGHTS-BASED LIMITATIONS

An extensive array of constitutionally-protected individual rights affect how government regulates in the interests of the public's health. Unlike the private sector (which does not generally owe individuals respect for their constitutional rights), government cannot infringe on fundamental individual rights without sufficient justification. Constitutional rights are not absolute, but rather are subject to constant balancing under differing rules and tests. The U.S. Supreme Court has developed different levels of scrutiny (i.e., standards) that it and other courts apply in assessing potential infringements depending on multifarious factors. These levels include:

Strict scrutiny—when fundamental rights (e.g., bodily privacy) or "suspect classes" (e.g., race, ethnicity, alienage, national origin) are at stake, government's action must (1) be narrowly tailored to serve a compelling government interest and (2) often represent the least restrictive means for accomplishing the objective. *Adarand Constructors, Inc. v. Pena*, 515 U.S. 200 (1995) (federal program that incentivized hiring subcontractors based on racial classification was subject to strict scrutiny). Whenever strict scrutiny is invoked, it is exceedingly difficult for government interests to prevail, and as a result, they are typically struck down by courts.

Take, for example, a public health regulation or policy that discriminates openly (or what courts sometimes refer to as "on its face") against persons on the basis of race by denying them access to public health services. Following a devastating hurricane in Galveston, Texas in September, 1900, essential supplies were reportedly distributed first to the city's white citizens; whatever was left each day was later handed out to African-Americans. *See* PATRICIA B. BIXEL & ELIZABETH H. TURNER, GALVESTON AND THE 1900 STORM: CATASTROPHE AND CATALYST 80 (2000). Such a law or policy is contrary to equal protection principles (discussed below). Absent a compelling governmental interest, it is unconstitutional.

Intermediate (or heightened) scrutiny—in other instances in which government actions or laws implicate individuals on grounds of gender, legitimacy of birth, or other bases, courts will assess whether there is a substantial relationship with important government interests. *See U.S. v. Virginia*, 518 U.S. 515 (1996) (state-run military institute's policy of admitting only male students was unconstitutional). Meeting this intermediate standard is easier than under strict scrutiny, but is still difficult when government action lacks a close nexus with public health objectives. In some cases, such as implementation of maternal health interventions, public health agencies may have sufficient justification for discriminating on the basis of gender. *See, e.g., Geduldig v. Aiello*, 417 U.S. 484 (1974) (California disability insurance program which failed to cover pregnancy did not violate equal protection claims because men and women are not similarly situated; Congress later prohibited pregnancy discrimination in 1978).

Rational basis scrutiny—in most other instances in which governments' actions infringe on individual rights or interests, a minimal level of scrutiny is applied. Government need only demonstrate that there is some rational basis for its expressed actions by showing a reasonable relationship to a legitimate government interest. *Vance v. Bradley*, 440 U.S. 93, 96–97 (1979) (government had a rational basis for implementing mandatory retirement age for Foreign Service employees which did not contravene principles of equal protection). Contrasted with strict scrutiny, whenever courts employ the rational basis test, they tend to defer to legislative or executive prerogatives consistent with separation of powers. So long as government can show some legitimate purpose, individual rights may be curtailed. As a result, public health laws measured under this standard usually survive scrutiny.

There are limited exceptions when the Supreme Court applies a more stringent form of rational basis review. In *City of Cleburne v. Cleburne Living Ctr., Inc.,* 473 U.S. 432 (1985), the Court invalidated a local zoning ordinance that attempted to restrict placement of a mental institution within a local community. It found there was no legitimate government interest underlying the ordinance that otherwise discriminated against persons with mental disabilities in violation of principles of equal protection.

B. BRIEF OVERVIEW OF SPECIFIC RIGHTS

The Constitution protects individuals and groups from unwarranted exercises of government, largely through the Bill of Rights and the 14th Amendment. These include fundamental rights to protect core freedoms (e.g., free speech), generalized rights to inhibit government oppression (e.g., due process), and rights designed to obviate government favoritism or discrimination (e.g., equal protection), as examined briefly below.

Public health practice may implicate 1st Amendment rights, specifically rights to free speech and expression, the right to assemble, and freedom of religion. These rights are held not only by individuals, but also corporations or other legally-recognized entities (e.g., associations, unions, and partnerships). The Supreme Court closely guards freedoms of speech and expression against government intrusion. *Tinker v. Des Moines Indep. Cmty. Sch. Dist.*, 393 U.S. 503 (1969); *Texas v. Johnson,* 491 U.S. 397 (1989). First Amendment protections for political, religious, and commercial speech range in their scope and application.

Political speech. Laws that directly impact political speech are subject to review under the Court's highest level of scrutiny. *Citizens United v. Federal Election Comm'n*, 558 U.S. 310 (2010). Political speech is "interactive communication concerning political change." *Buckley v. American Constitutional Law Found., Inc.*, 525 U.S. 182, 186 (1999) (citing *Meyer v. Grant*, 486 U.S. 414, 422 (1988)). This includes not only politics and candidates in general, but also "structures and forms of government, the manner in which government is operated . . . , and all such matters relating to political processes." *Mills v. Alabama*, 384 U.S. 214, 218–19 (1966). So long as such speech is covered (that is, it is not false, misleading, defamatory, implicating national security threats, or other limited contexts), the 1st Amendment assures individuals their right to speak publicly or privately.

Commercial speech. Government infringements on commercial speech, or "expressions related solely to the economic interests of the speaker and its audience," garner their own unique review. *Central Hudson Gas & Elec. Corp. v. Public Serv. Comm'n of N.Y.,* 447 U.S. 557 (1980). Infringements on commercial speech emanate typically from government attempts to (1) limit the time, place, and manner of advertising of specific, lawful products (e.g., tobacco) generally or to specific audiences (e.g., minors); or (2) require commercial entities to provide truthful information (e.g., warnings about known or potential product harms) or counter information (e.g., calorie labeling on menus). In such cases, the Supreme Court assesses each potential infringement typically under a 4–part test set forth in its *Central Hudson* decision, discussed later in Chapter 8.

Freedom of assembly. Pursuant to the 1st Amendment, individuals also have the right to gather, or assemble, for lawful purposes subject to reasonable restrictions. Freedom of assembly may not extend to group activities that negatively impact the community or the public's health. For example, political protesters who erected tents and accumulated garbage and human waste in New York City in 2011 were lawfully dispersed by the City and park owner to maintain hygiene and public safety. *In re Waller v. City of New York,* 933 N.Y.S.2d 541 (N.Y. Sup. Ct. 2011). Government may impose such measures provided restrictions are narrowly tailored, serve a compelling government interest, and provide alternative channels for individuals to communicate or associate. *Clark v.*

Community for Creative Non-Violence, 468 U.S. 288 (1984).

Freedom of religion. The 1st Amendment Establishment Clause ["Congress shall make no law respecting an establishment of religion . . ."] and Free Exercise Clause ["or prohibiting the free exercise thereof . . ."] protect religious freedoms. They work in tandem to prohibit government from endorsing or "establishing" specific religious faiths and support individuals' freedom to practice their chosen religion. In many ways, these 2 facets of religious freedom are compatible to the extent they allow individuals to believe as they choose without governmental interference or influence through support for 1 religion over another. In the public health context, however, sometimes they are at odds, as explained further in relation to vaccination laws and policies in Chapter 4.

Due process. Additional rights often implicated through public health powers include principles of due process. Pursuant to the 5th Amendment (and later the 14th Amendment, which applies the Bill of Rights to the states) government shall not "deprive any person of life, liberty, or property, without due process of law." There are 2 major types of due process protections: procedural and substantive. Prior to or coextensive with deprivations of life, liberty, or property, government must provide individuals with some procedural steps or assurances (e.g., notice, right to counsel, right to an appeal). The level and extent of process due depend on the scope and extent of deprivation of rights involved. *Mathews v. Eldridge*, 424 U.S. 319 (1976).

Substantive due process requires government to have a sufficient justification for depriving individuals' life, liberty, or property interests. ERWIN CHEMERINSKY, CONSTITUTIONAL LAW: PRINCIPLES AND POLICIES 558 (4th ed. 2011). Any time government infringes on these basic interests in arbitrary, vague, or capricious ways, courts may find that such infringements violate substantive due process. *See, e.g., Foucha v. Louisiana*, 504 U.S. 71 (1992) (Louisiana law that commits a person acquitted from insanity charges violates substantive due process). Additional rights flow from court interpretations of the breadth of "life, liberty, or property," such as the right to travel, discussed below.

Right to travel. Although the Constitution does not expressly provide for a right to travel, it is firmly embedded in fundamental liberties (*see* CHEMERINSKY, CONSTITUTIONAL LAW, at 879), and the Privileges and Immunities Clause, which helps assure state citizens share similar benefits and protections in other states. U.S. CONST. art. IV, § 2, cl. 1. This Clause is a primary basis for protecting persons against (1) the erection of "actual barriers to interstate movement" and (2) disparate treatment for intrastate travelers. *Doe v. Miller,* 405 F.3d 700, 711 (8th Cir. 2005). Government cannot prevent individuals from entering or leaving a state (without strong justification), mistreat visitors to a state, and must extend similar benefits to persons who choose to reside in a state. *Saenz v. Roe,* 526 U.S. 489, 499 (1999).

While the right to travel is extensive, it can be restricted via government. A Florida law that required sex offenders to notify law enforcement when they permanently or temporarily change their address was approved against a right to travel challenge in *Doe v. Moore*, 410 F.3d 1337, 1348 (11th Cir. 2005). The 11th Circuit Court of Appeals found that there was a compelling state interest in "preventing future sexual offenses and alerting local law enforcement and citizens to the whereabouts of those that could reoffend." *Id.* In the same year, the 8th Circuit upheld an Iowa sex offender law that limited travel "to protect the health and safety of the citizens." *Miller*, 405 F.3d at 705. *See also Burman v. Streeval*, No. 4:11CV0569, 2011 WL 3562999 (N.D. Ohio Aug. 11, 2011) (prisoner's segregation for not consenting to TB test does not infringe his right to travel).

Equal protection. Principles of equal protection, derived from the 14th Amendment, require similar treatment for like individuals. They apply automatically to state and local governments via the language of the 14th Amendment, and to the federal government through the 5th Amendment. *See, e.g., Bolling v. Sharpe,* 347 U.S. 497 (1954) (federal government must adhere to same equal protection requirements as states, specifically concerning school desegregation, to avoid a denial of due process under the 5th Amendment).

Equal protection may be invoked by public health laws or policies that classify specific persons or groups. People with certain conditions or living in particular areas may be targeted for government public health interventions. Older adults may be entitled to special services not provided to younger persons. Children may benefit from public health programs for which adults are left out. Neither of these examples presents equal protection violations so long as government has some rational basis for distinguishing individuals in the interests of the public's health.

However, when classifications are based on "suspect classes" (e.g., race, ethnicity, nonmarital children) or other questionable grounds (gender), the level of scrutiny ramps up (as discussed above), and the intervention may be found contrary to principles of equal protection. CHEMERINSKY, CONSTITUTIONAL LAW, at 684–801. Some laws violate equal protection because they openly authorize discrimination on their face. For example, a state quarantine order that applied solely to persons of Asian descent, even though the communicable disease targeted by the order was transmissible among all races, is patently unconstitutional. *Jew Ho v. Williamson*, 103 F. 10 (N.D. Cal. 1900).

Other laws are neutral as stated, but discriminatory in their administration. Sometimes "the impact of a law may be so clearly discriminatory as to allow no other explanation than that it was adopted for impermissible purposes."

CHEMERINSKY, CONSTITUTIONAL LAW, at 732. Concerning laws which have a disparate impact, discriminatory purposes (and likely effects) must be proven for an equal protection violation to arise. *Id.* at 713, 730. For example, in *Village of Arlington Heights v. Metropolitan Hous. Dev. Corp.*, 429 U.S. 252 (1977), a city council in Illinois refused to rezone an area of land to allow low and moderate income housing construction. African Americans alleged the zoning policy effectively denied them access to the community. The Supreme Court agreed: "[s]ometimes a clear pattern, unexplainable on grounds other than race, emerges from the effect of the state action even when the governing legislation appears neutral on its face." *Id.* at 266.

Equal protection principles are reflected in multiple federal, state, and local laws addressing discrimination on many fronts. The federal Civil Rights Act (CRA) of 1964 bans discrimination on the grounds of race, ethnicity, and national or religious origins (as we well as sex in many, but not all, sectors). Pub. L. No. 88–352, 78 Stat. 241 (codified as amended in scattered sections of 42 U.S.C. (2009)). Private membership clubs and public international organizations, for example, may discriminate on the basis of sex. EEOC COMPLIANCE MANUAL § 2–III(B)(4) (2009).

CRA's protections can advance some public health objectives. For example, in *EEOC v. Houston Funding,* 717 F.3d 425 (5th Cir. 2013), a woman who was fired for lactating was successful in her claim against her employer for sexual discrimination under CRA Title VII (as amended by the Pregnancy Discrimination Act of 1978, 42 U.S.C. § 2000e(k) (2008)). Additional protections for breastfeeding women are provided via the ACA, Pub. L. No. 111–148, § 4207 (amending 29 U.S.C. § 207), as well as state laws. In combination, these laws help promote maternal and child health by eliminating discrimination against women.

Rights to privacy. Rights to privacy extend from multiple parts of the Constitution and are constantly raised through public health policies and practices. There are 3 primary types of privacy: bodily, decisional, and informational. Anita L. Allen, *Taking Liberties: Privacy, Private Choice, and Social Contract Theory*, 56 U. CIN. L. REV. 461, 464–66 (1987). *Bodily* privacy extends principally from liberty principles inherent in due process as well as freedoms from unreasonable searches and seizures via the 4th Amendment. As discussed in Chapter 4, respect for bodily privacy prevents government from forcing an autonomous individual to receive specific treatment or undergo intrusive public health screening and testing without compelling justification.

Decisional privacy concerns individuals' interests in making core, personal decisions about their health or other status without unwarranted governmental interference. This facet of privacy supports persons' interests in making reproductive or other medical choices, determining the extent of medical or other care they desire, and deciding how best to parent their children. *See Prince v.*

Massachusetts, 321 U.S. 158 (1944) (appealing child labor conviction on parental rights basis). This latter "right to parent" arises concerning public health programs that mitigate parental choices (*see* Chapter 4 for additional discussion).

Rights to *informational* privacy apply to persons' sensitive, private information, notably including health data. A bevy of privacy statutes and regulations govern the access, use, and disclosure of one's personally-identifiable medical information, but constitutional protections via due process are fairly lax. Provided government can demonstrate a rational basis for accessing or requesting identifiable data to promote or protect the public's health, as well as reasonable security measures, such uses are constitutionally permitted. *See Whalen v. Roe*, 429 U.S. 589 (1977) (discussed in Chapter 7).

Freedom from cruel and unusual punishment. The 8th Amendment prohibits government from inflicting "cruel and unusual punishment," based on evolving standards set in part by the Supreme Court. *Roper v. Simmons*, 543 U.S. 551 (2005). Though more often implicated in criminal cases related to the death penalty (*see Stanford v. Kentucky*, 492 U.S. 361 (1989)), and other punitive cases, the 8th Amendment also applies to some public health measures. In *Estelle v. Gamble*, 429 U.S. 97 (1976), the Court found that the prohibition of cruel and unusual punishment supports government's provision of medical care to prisoners. *Id.* at 103.

Respect for constitutional rights is often synergistic with advancing the public's health. However, some constitutionally-protected rights may deter or defeat interventions designed to prevent excess morbidity and mortality. These include constitutional protections favoring the right to bear arms and limiting government takings of private property discussed below.

Right to bear arms. The 2nd Amendment guarantees that the "right to keep and bear arms . . . shall not be infringed." This strongly-held right directly collides with public health interventions designed to curb gun-related violence and death in the U.S. Epic political and constitutional battles arise over the balance between efforts to prevent gun violence nationally and individuals' interests in owning and using firearms. IOM & NAT'L RESEARCH COUNCIL, PRIORITIES FOR RESEARCH TO REDUCE THE THREAT OF FIREARM-RELATED VIOLENCE (2013).

In *District of Columbia v. Heller*, 554 U.S. 570 (2008), the Supreme Court held that the District's attempt to prohibit the possession and use of handguns is unconstitutional, but allowed: (1) "prohibitions on possession of firearms by felons and the mentally ill;" (2) "laws forbidding the carrying of firearms in sensitive places such as schools and government buildings;" (3) "conditions and qualifications on the commercial sale of firearms;" and (4) prohibitions on the "carrying of 'dangerous and unusual weapons.'" *Id.* at 626–27. Two years later, the Court rejected a similar local hand gun law in Chicago, clarifying that the 2nd Amendment applies to the states through the 14th Amendment. *McDonald v. City of Chicago,* 130 S. Ct. 3020, 3050 (2010).

Takings. Pursuant to its powers of eminent domain, government can take private property for public use. However, the 5th Amendment requires that any government taking be accompanied by "just compensation." Stated simply, government cannot take private property for public use without paying for it, subject to determinations of its economic value. As discussed in Chapter 9, compensating owners is not required when government legitimately exercises its power to abate public health nuisances.

Furthermore, what qualifies as a "public use" varies, but most definitely includes public health purposes. For example, a local government may justifiably take privately-held resources during a public health emergency so long as it pays for them later. The Supreme Court also recognizes a broader realm of qualifying uses. In *Kelo v. City of New London,* 545 U.S. 469 (2005), New London, Connecticut addressed "economic distress" in its downtown and waterfront areas by taking private land for redevelopment. *Id.* at 472. The Court upheld the City's plan, acknowledging that economic development alone can actually constitute a "public purpose." *Id.* at 485.

C. VOLUNTARY, MANDATORY & COMPULSORY POWERS

Each of these individual rights or protections may be implicated and assessed under a different level of scrutiny as applied to specific public health powers, which may be classified as voluntary, mandatory, or compulsory in nature.

Voluntary interventions refer generally to measures that elicit the participation of individuals or groups acting on their own volition. Lawful efforts to address communicable diseases, for example, may include education campaigns. *See, e.g., Doe v. Irwin*, 615 F.2d 1162 (6th Cir. 1980) (family planning center offering voluntary sex education classes and contraceptives to minors); *see also* Chapter 8. They may also include vaccine drives, testing or screening programs, and treatment options. *See, e.g., Parents United for Better Sch., Inc. v. School Dist. of Phila. Bd. of Edu.*, 148 F.3d 260 (3rd Cir. 1998) (optional condom distribution program approved at a public school); *see also* Chapter 4. In each instance, individuals seek information or public health services based on their own choice, often reflected through their informed consent (such as prior to testing or treatment). Use of voluntary public health powers is consistent with public health ethics (*see* Chapter 1) and highly favored in public health practice so long as they are efficacious.

Mandatory public health powers raise the stakes. When legally authorized, practitioners may implement public health interventions that no

longer seek the voluntary actions of individuals.
Rather, they set conditions on participation to
encourage or require individuals or groups to
protect the public's health to avoid penalties or loss
of privileges. Requiring citizens to be vaccinated or
else be fined, as described in section D, below, is an
example. Others include testing, screening, and
treatment programs that mandate individual
compliance subject to varying conditions, such as
receipt of treatment or other services. Participation
in a treatment program may be conditioned on one's
avoidance of more intrusive public health measures,
such as isolation (*see* Chapter 4). In each of these
and other instances, mandatory public health
powers are often challenged based on infringements
of individual freedoms and rights even though
individuals ultimately retain the choice of
participating.

With the exercise of *compulsory* public health
powers, individual choice is no longer an option, nor
is government offering the chance to participate to
avoid penalties or receive valued services or
benefits. One's participation will be garnered by
force of varying magnitude as necessary.
Compulsory interventions require individuals to
participate or change their behaviors irrespective of
their consent. In the early 1900s, New York City
public health officials went door-to-door to forcibly
vaccinate adults against smallpox or other
infectious diseases. Implementation of the
Chamberlain-Kahn Act of 1918, 42 U.S.C. §§ 24–
25e, ch. 143, ch. XV, sec. 3–4e (1918), as amended in
1938, involved the forcible detention of known or

suspected prostitutes for treatment and study. The
Act was repealed in 1944. *Id.* at ch. 373 tit. XIII,
§ 1313.

A vestige of public health practice from bygone
eras, compulsory public health powers are seldom
used today because they run counter to public
health ethics and significantly infringe on
individual liberties. Exercises of compulsory powers
may fail to survive constitutional scrutiny even if
government has compelling interests (often because
there are less restrictive alternatives available).
Yet, examples of the use of compulsory powers in
the control of infectious diseases remain. For
example, forcible testing of persons charged with
criminal transmission of HIV may be allowed to
determine whether the individual has the condition
and protect others who may have been exposed. *See
In re Multimedia KSDK, Inc.,* 581 N.E.2d 911 (Ill.
App. Ct. 1991).

Social distancing measures, including quarantine,
isolation, and curfews (discussed in Chapter 4), may
be implemented voluntarily, but when necessary,
government can require affected persons to adhere
to such measures, especially in public health
emergencies. *See* TURNING POINT MODEL STATE PUB.
HEALTH ACT § 5–101 (2003). Compulsory powers
may also be used to protect the health of minors,
prisoners, or others pursuant to *parens patriae*
powers (discussed in Chapter 2).

D. BALANCING INDIVIDUAL & COMMUNITY INTERESTS

At the heart of public health law are struggles to determine the point at which government authority to promote the population's health must yield to individual constitutional rights. For much of this nation's history, this balance was firmly weighted in favor of public health interventions. Countless court decisions through the early 20th century found in favor of state or local governments seeking to protect the public's health, sometimes to the detriment of individual rights. James G. Hodge, Jr., *The Role of New Federalism and Public Health Law*, 12 J.L. & HEALTH 309 (1998). Courts justified these decisions in part by the strong need for public health measures to control infectious and chronic conditions for which there were no cures and scant, incomplete, or inaccurate epidemiologic data. Public health actors were granted significant deference to stymie significant threats to the health and economy of the community.

Yet other legal factors were also at play. In the early 1900s, Congress and the Supreme Court had yet to fully recognize the application of the Bill of Rights to state and local governments. CHEMERINSKY, CONSTITUTIONAL LAW, at 511–19. Thus, for example, the protections of the 1st Amendment did not fully apply to state and local governments via the "incorporation doctrine" until 1925. *Gitlow v. N.Y.*, 268 U.S. 652, 666 (1925). Furthermore, courts' deference to public health legislation (through separation of powers principles)

and respect for varying authorities among the levels
of government (via federalism) were different.

Each of these issues is on display in one of the
most famous and oft-cited public health cases in
Supreme Court jurisprudence, *Jacobson v.
Massachusetts*, 197 U.S. 11 (1905). The
Commonwealth of Massachusetts legislature
enacted a law empowering local boards of health to
require the vaccination of residents if necessary for
the public health or safety. Facing a potential
outbreak of smallpox, the City of Cambridge Board
of Health issued a vaccination requirement in 1902
that all persons be inoculated or face a $5 fine.

Henning Jacobson, a local reverend, refused the
smallpox vaccination. He was convicted by a local
court and ordered to pay the fine. On appeal, the
Massachusetts Supreme Judicial Court upheld the
conviction. Jacobson took his case to the U.S.
Supreme Court, arguing that Cambridge's
compulsory vaccination law was "unreasonable,
arbitrary, and oppressive," and thus "hostile to the
inherent right of every freeman to care for his own
body and health." *Id.* at 26. His claim was grounded
mainly in constitutional liberty interests which, he
asserted, supported natural rights of persons to
bodily integrity and decisional privacy (although he
also argued on grounds of equal protection and
other legal bases).

Rejecting Jacobson's appeal, the Supreme Court
adopted a narrower view of individual liberty under
substantive due process while taking a more
community-oriented approach in which citizens owe

duties to each other and society as a whole. Justice John M. Harlan, writing for the Court, stated:

> [T]he liberty secured by the Constitution . . . does not import an absolute right in each person to be, at all times and in all circumstances, wholly freed from restraint. There are manifold restraints to which every person is necessarily subject for the common good. On any other basis organized society could not exist with safety to its members. . . . *Id.*

Under the social compact theory advanced by the Court, a community has the right to implement public health requirements to protect itself against threatening diseases consistent with state police powers. The legacy of *Jacobson* is seen most clearly in the Court's defense of the breadth and necessity of public health authority under the police power (discussed in Chapter 2).

Yet the Court continued its analysis, offering a seminal change in the prior balance of police power authorities and individual rights. While acknowledging the extent of public health authority, Justice Harlan recognized specific limits to such exercises. As explained by Lawrence Gostin, utilizing state police powers in support of vaccination requirements or other compulsory public health initiatives is constitutionally permissible when exercised in conformity with the principles of:

(1) *public health necessity*—police powers used in the interests of communal health must be justified,

and not exercised in arbitrary ways beyond what is reasonably required for the safety of the public;

(2) *reasonable means*—there must be some reasonable relationship between the public health intervention and the achievement of a legitimate public health objective that does not plainly invade individual rights;

(3) *proportionality*—public health powers that are arbitrary and oppressive in particular cases may require judicial intervention to prevent injustices or "absurd consequence[s]." *Id*. Even efficacious public health interventions may be unconstitutional if they are onerous or unfair; and

(4) *harm avoidance*—no compulsory public health measure should pose direct risks to specific persons with known adverse reactions. Thus, while persons may be required to be vaccinated for the common good, those who can demonstrate they are "unfit subjects" for vaccination because of the potential for adverse health consequences may not be subjected to the intervention. *Id*. at 12. Jacobson argued that he was not fit for vaccination, but the Court found he failed to present sufficient medical evidence in support of his claim. Requiring a person to be immunized despite knowing harm, concluded the Court, would be "cruel and inhuman in the last degree." *Id*. at 39; *see* LAWRENCE O. GOSTIN, PUBLIC HEALTH LAW: POWER, DUTY, RESTRAINT 126–28 (2d ed. 2008).

Jacobson stands firmly for the proposition that police powers authorize states to require vaccination for the public good, but such powers must be exercised reasonably consistent with due process or other individual rights. Yet, there is another side to the case that reflects the Court's appreciation of structural constitutional constraints at the time.

Concerning Jacobson's rights-based claims, attorneys for the Commonwealth of Massachusetts argued in essence that the state and its legislative bodies have: (1) unquestionable powers and duties to protect the public's health (to which courts must defer); and (2) reasonably determined that smallpox vaccinations in affected communities further the public's health. In prior cases with similar facts, courts typically adjudicated in favor of government. However, the Commonwealth also recognized the nature and force of Jacobson's objections. The "antivaccination" movement during this period was vocal and strong (even if the minority). As well, the Cambridge Board of Health regulation failed to specify its lawful support. *See* Wendy E. Parmet et al., *Individual Rights versus the Public's Health— 100 Years after Jacobson v. Massachusetts*, 352 NEW ENG. J. MED. 652 (2005).

The Commonwealth attempted to counter Jacobson's liberty-based claim with arguments grounded in structural principles of constitutional law, including separation of powers, federalism, and social contract theory under the Massachusetts' state constitution. Concerning separation of powers, the Commonwealth argued that courts cannot contravene public health legislative judgments unless such were utterly arbitrary and unreasonable. Neither the Cambridge vaccination requirement nor the lower court's refusal to allow Jacobson's evidence of his fitness for vaccination was improper in light of the exercise of the state's overwhelming police powers.

Massachusetts' attorneys intimated that courts should not question the rational judgments of a local legislative body acting under a proper delegation of police power from the Commonwealth, which the Supreme Court acknowledged. "[The] [C]ourt would usurp the functions of another branch of government if it adjudged, as a matter of law, that the mode adopted under the sanction of the state, to protect the people at large was arbitrary and not justified by the necessities of the case." *Jacobson*, 197 U.S. at 28. Both the Court and the Commonwealth agreed in principle that when the legislature has spoken, it is entitled to significant judicial deference (even if constitutional rights are implicated). As Justice Harlan noted, "no court . . . is justified in disregarding the action of the legislature simply because in its . . . opinion [a] particular method was—perhaps or possibly—not the best." *Id*. at 35.

Principles of federalism also come into play. Though these principles undulate over time between state sovereignty and federal supremacy, in 1905 they were pointed firmly in the direction of the states. The Court acceded. "The safety and health of the people of Massachusetts are, in the first instance, for that Commonwealth to guard and protect. They are matters that do not ordinarily concern the national government." *Id.* at 38. It, however, also recognized its own judicial role. "While this [C]ourt should guard with firmness every right appertaining to life, liberty, or property . . . , it is of the last importance that it should not invade the domain of local authority except when it is plainly necessary to do so . . . ." *Id.* Clearly the Court respected principles of federalism in support of states' public health powers, but retained its authority to arbitrate potential constitutional violations of individual freedoms.

Finally, the Supreme Court acknowledged the Commonwealth's presentation of principles of communal responsibility inherent in social contract theory. The Massachusetts constitution sets forth "as a fundamental principle of the social compact that the whole people covenants with each other and that all should be governed by certain laws for the common good," *id.* at 27, notably including public health laws.

These structural principles (separation of powers, federalism, and social compact theory) shed greater light on how and why *Jacobson* was decided. Sovereign states are instituted to, among other things, protect the public's health for the benefit of their citizens. The Commonwealth used its broad police powers in the pursuit of protecting the community. The federal judicial branch must respect that exercise consistent with separation of powers and federalism. To the extent the Commonwealth's actions furthered the public's

health,   they   counter-balance   potential
infringements of individual constitutional rights.

As   constitutional   norms   change,   these
observations may no longer govern review of modern
public health cases involving the juxtaposition of
state police powers and individual rights. Yet,
Jacobson must be read more broadly than it is oft-
cited in support of (1) government regulation of
persons in the interests of public health and safety,
(2) limitations on individual liberty interests as
needed to protect communal health, and (3) various
school   vaccination   requirements,   isolation,
quarantine,   fluoridation,   and other public health
measures.

The true legacy of *Jacobson* is its historical and
modern guidance on when and how to balance the
states' use of public health powers with individual
rights and interests.   The case remains good law
because of the Court's essential recognition that
protecting the public's health is synergistic with
respecting individual liberties. *See* James G. Hodge,
Jr.,   *Jacobson   v.   Massachusetts: Alternate
Perspectives*, 33 J.L. MED. & ETHICS 26 (Supp. 2005).

Understanding the breadth of the field of public
health law coupled with the source, scope, and
limits of government's public health powers provides
an appropriate backdrop for further study. In Part
2, specific legal authority to prevent and control
public health conditions, including communicable
and chronic diseases as well as avoidable injuries

and corresponding deaths, is examined. At all levels
of government, these conditions not only justify the
use of significant public health powers, but also
raise some of the most difficult tradeoffs with
respect to individual rights and structural norms.

PART 2

LEGAL AUTHORITY TO PREVENT & CONTROL PUBLIC HEALTH CONDITIONS

Threats to the public's health are numerous and diverse. Long-standing (e.g., TB) and emerging (e.g., H7N9 avian flu) communicable diseases remain a scourge of populations. Chronic conditions, including heart disease, cancers, and diabetes, afflict millions of Americans. Preventable injuries and concomitant deaths negatively impact or cut short the lives of children and adults across the globe. Core to the mission of public health is the mitigation of the effects of these and other threats to individual and community health.

American government at all levels has available numerous, traditional, and long-standing powers to address public health risks. It may exercise these public health powers directly, or defer to partners in the private sector for their execution or assistance. So long as these powers are properly grounded in constitutional authorities and limits, the slate of legal options is extensive. When wielded in the interests of community wellness, public health legal powers can be an effective tool for improving outcomes. However, if exercised (1) with impunity for individual liberties or other constitutionally-protected rights, (2) counter to core principles of public health ethics, or (3) in politically insensitive ways, public health authorities lack legal and practical justifications for their actions.

This Part discusses the legal bases for interventions to address major challenges to communal health stemming from communicable diseases (Chapter 4), chronic conditions (Chapter 5), and injuries and deaths (Chapter 6). Public health powers used to address some conditions, such as the power to test, screen, vaccinate, or treat communicable diseases, may equally apply to other illnesses, such as cancers. However, some of these powers are used almost exclusively in response to a particular type of threat (e.g., use of expedited partner therapy to address sexually-transmitted diseases).

Execution of public health powers to address any condition requires careful tradeoffs between individual freedoms and community needs. Therein lies the need for constant balancing of these respective interests at the core of public health law. As in Part 1, this theme is revisited in many contexts throughout the illustration of public health powers and their related impacts on individual rights.

CHAPTER 4

PREVENTING & TREATING COMMUNICABLE CONDITIONS

The global history of public health practice is intrinsically tied to the prevention and control of communicable diseases. From the founding of the U.S. to modern times, curbing the threat of illnesses spread between and among individuals has been a constant objective. Even as the mission of public health has expanded to assuring the conditions for people to be healthy (discussed in Chapter 1), controlling the spread of communicable diseases remains a focal point for federal, tribal, state, and local public health agencies. In pursuit of this objective they are equipped with preventive tools, techniques, and data thanks to considerable advances in public health surveillance and control practices. Key to the prevention and control of communicable diseases, however, is the law.

Many legal interventions to respond to communicable disease threats are available, but they come with associated tradeoffs. Intermixed with some of the most ancient of communal health authorities (e.g., isolation and quarantine) are relatively new public health powers (e.g., directly-observed therapy) that together comprise the bastion of public health abilities to address communicable conditions. Exploration of these powers and associated trade-offs begins with an assessment of the scope and impact of communicable conditions on human health in the U.S. and abroad.

A. COMMUNICABLE CONDITIONS— DEFINED

A communicable condition is defined broadly as "an illness caused by an infectious agent or its toxins that occurs through the direct or indirect transmission of the infectious agent or its products" from different sources. N.Y.C., N.Y., HEALTH CODE tit. 24, § 11.01 (2010). Defining communicable diseases is easy. Predicting their spread (a main thrust of epidemiology) and controlling their impacts on populations are not.

Many communicable diseases are transmitted between humans through air-borne agents (e.g., influenza), casual contact (e.g., chicken pox), from mother to child (e.g., HIV), or via the transfer of blood or other bodily fluids from unprotected sexual contact (e.g., gonorrhea). Some infectious diseases are contracted through other living vectors such as animals (e.g., rabies), insects (e.g., Lyme disease), or plants/fungi (e.g., Valley Fever). Environmental sources such as water (e.g., cryptosporidium) and food (e.g., salmonella) also serve as dominant modes of transmission of infectious diseases.

Communicable conditions present enormous public health challenges. Some infectious agents may be primary bioterrorism threats (e.g., smallpox, anthrax, tularemia, plague, ebola, and botulism). NAT'L ACADS. & DHS, BIOLOGICAL ATTACK: HUMAN PATHOGENS, BIOTOXINS, AND AGRICULTURAL

THREATS (2004). As discussed further in Chapter 10, their appearance in any individual or group in the U.S. garners immediate and substantial public health investigation and control efforts because of the likelihood of bioterrorist activity.

Other diseases that transmit easily between humans can also wreak havoc on populations. The 1918–19 "Spanish flu" pandemic killed upwards of 100 million people globally. JOHN M. BARRY, THE GREAT INFLUENZA: THE STORY OF THE DEADLIEST PANDEMIC IN HISTORY 397 (2005). According to the World Health Organization (WHO), the 2009/2010 H1N1 pandemic flu infected millions and killed thousands worldwide. WHO, EVOLUTION OF A PANDEMIC: A(H1N1) 2009 (2013). Even annual flu outbreaks are lethal, lending to preventable mortality ranging from 3,000 ~ 49,000 deaths per year in the U.S. alone. CDC, *Estimates of Deaths Associated with Seasonal Influenza—U.S., 1976–2007,* 59 MMWR 1057 (Aug. 27, 2010) (statistics based on 30 years of CDC surveillance data).

Many infectious conditions are less easily transmitted, but still necessitate public health attention. In 2011 alone, approximately 8.7 million people globally contracted TB, multi-drug resistant (MDR-) TB, or extreme drug resistant (XDR-) TB, and nearly 1.5 million people died from TB-related causes. WHO, GLOBAL TB REPORT 9 (2012). Dwindling resources and continued global migration suggest more persons may contract and perish from this centuries-old disease (once known as consumption) in the years ahead. Localized outbreaks of TB still occur in the U.S., mostly in urban environments. Kiren Mitruka et al., *TB Outbreak Investigations in the U.S., 2002–2008*, 17 EMERGING INFECTIOUS DISEASES 425 (2011).

Sexually-transmitted infections (STIs) present significant, often undetected risks internationally and in the U.S. Since its emergence in the early 1980s, HIV/AIDS has claimed over 25 million lives globally. WHO, HIV/AIDS: FACT SHEET NO. 360 (2012). CDC estimates over a million people are living with HIV/AIDS in the U.S.; nearly 20% do not know they are infected. CDC, *Monitoring Selected National HIV Prevention and Care Objectives by Surveillance Data*, 17 HIV SURVEILLANCE SUPPLEMENTAL REP. 6 (2012). Another 50,000 persons in the U.S. contracted the disease in 2013. CDC, FACT SHEET: NEW HIV INFECTIONS IN THE U.S. (2012).

The most common STI is genital human papillomavirus (HPV). Approximately 80 million Americans are infected. Nearly all sexually-active men and women will get at least 1 type of HPV at some point in their lives. Though the condition is largely asymptomatic in most persons, some strains can lead to genital warts, and more significantly, cervical and other cancers. CDC, GENITAL HPV INFECTION—FACT SHEET (2013); CDC, *STD Treatment Guidelines, 2010*, 59 MMWR 1, 69–70 (Dec. 17, 2010).

Hundreds of thousands of individuals are infected with 2 other STIs, gonorrhea or Chlamydia. Nearly 14,000 new infections of syphilis were also reported in 2011. CDC, FACT SHEET: STD TRENDS IN THE U.S.: 2011 NATIONAL DATA FOR CHLAMYDIA, GONORRHEA, AND SYPHILIS (2013). Left untreated, each of these STIs can lead to significant long-term disabilities, including cancers and infertility, or death.

Improper food handling practices and questionable sanitation from farms to factories also contribute significantly to the spread of infectious diseases. Nearly 20,000 lab-confirmed cases of food-related illness were reported to CDC in 2011. The actual number of cases is likely many times higher. Salmonella poisonings alone led to 2,290 hospitalizations and 29 deaths that same year. CDC, *Vital Signs: Incidence and Trends of Infection with Pathogens Transmitted Commonly Through Food,* 60 MMWR 749 (June 10, 2011).

Water-borne infectious agents, including the sometimes deadly cryptosporidium, cause hundreds of infections each year. They arise predominantly through exposure to microorganisms in recreational water or through contaminants in public or private water supplies. CDC, *Surveillance for Waterborne Disease Outbreaks and Other Health Events,* 60 MMWR 1 (Sept. 23, 2011). In 1993 undetected cryptosporidium contaminations in the city water supply of Milwaukee, Wisconsin led to 69 deaths. Phaedra S. Corso et al., *Cost of Illness in the 1993 Waterborne Cryptosporidium Outbreak, Milwaukee, Wisconsin,* 9 EMERGING INFECTIOUS DISEASES 426, 430 (2003); *Markweise v. Peck Foods Corp.,* 556 N.W.2d 326 (Wis. Ct. App. 1996) (resulting litigation against the city and others was dismissed due to failure to provide advance notice of claim).

Whether spread via air-borne, casual or sexual contact, or other vectors, communicable conditions continue to challenge the public's health despite victories over many diseases that once plagued populations (e.g., polio, measles, mumps, and rubella). U.S. public health authorities rely on their legal authority to engage in a series of voluntary, mandatory, or compulsory measures (discussed in Chapter 3) to prevent or control infectious diseases, as set forth in the sections below.

B. TESTING & SCREENING

Public health powers to test and screen for communicable conditions are authorized generally or in relation to varied conditions via statute or regulation in all states and many localities. Though often conflated, testing and screening are different. Individuals are subject to diagnostic tests (or procedures) to ascertain the presence or absence of a particular condition. Screening involves the application of specific tests to the population. Ronald Bayer et al., *HIV Antibody Screening: An Ethical Framework for Evaluating Proposed Programs*, 256 JAMA 1768, 1768 (1986). Hence, a person may be a member of a high-risk population recommended for *screening* and thus receive a diagnostic *test* for a specified condition.

Multiple practical factors militate whether public health authorities may engage testing or screening programs or initiatives, including their affordability, accuracy, efficacy, ethicality, and potential for positive interventions based on results. *See, e.g.,* Bob Ortega, *FDA to Scrutinize HPV Test Linked to False Readings*, ARIZ. REPUBLIC, July 31, 2013, at A1 (FDA to review laboratory use of specific HPV test based on reported high rates of false positive results).

Testing and screening programs that (1) provide pre- and post-counseling, (2) seek voluntary compliance expressed through advance informed consent, (3) shun coercive tactics, and (4) avoid unwarranted classification of protected groups are legally acceptable. For example, the U.S. Preventative Services Task Force (USPSTF) issues a series of national guidelines determining whom should be tested for varied communicable conditions, all of which are followed at the discretion of health care workers and their patients. USPSTF, THE GUIDE TO CLINICAL PREVENTIVE SERVICES v (2012).

Still, voluntary testing and screening programs can raise legal concerns over privacy. In 2006, CDC adjusted its national recommendation for the administration of HIV/AIDS tests to include all persons ages 13–64 seeking routine physicals or other treatment. CDC, *Revised Recommendations for HIV Testing of Adults, Adolescents, and Pregnant Women in Health-Care Settings*, 55 MMWR 1, 7 (Sept. 22, 2006). Its recommendation was coupled with an "opt-out" feature, meaning testing would be done automatically unless an individual expressly rejected it. In 2013, President

Obama expressed continued support for the voluntary testing of Americans to facilitate advance detection and treatment of HIV. Elise Viebeck, *Obama Urges Widespread Testing for HIV*, HILL, June 27, 2013.

While some have expressed privacy concerns related to this opt-out mode of implementation, CDC's recommendation reflected a watershed adjustment in national HIV/AIDS strategy following nearly 2 decades of various testing and screening programs focused on high-risk groups (e.g., homosexual men, pregnant women, injecting drug users, sex offenders). IOM, HIV SCREENING AND ACCESS TO CARE: EXPLORING BARRIERS AND FACILITATORS TO EXPANDED HIV TESTING (2010). These types of screening efforts were challenged legally based on their potential to infringe the bodily and informational privacy of at-risk individuals (*see In re Juveniles A, B, C, D, E*, 847 P.2d 455 (Wash. 1993) (HIV screening of juvenile and adult sex offenders is not a violation of constitutional right to privacy). Additional challenges arose over the use of named-based reporting of test results to local, state, and federal public health authorities. *See Middlebrooks v. State Bd. of Health*, 710 So. 2d 891 (Ala. 1998) (state statute requiring name-based reporting of HIV/AIDS patients by physicians does not violate informational privacy rights) (discussed further in Chapter 7).

Other legal issues stem from testing or screening programs. Like most states, Minnesota public health authorities oversee a screening program to search for initial, potential genetic or other conditions among newborns. *See* Charlotte Tucker, *Fifty Years of Screening: Testing Newborns Can Prevent Lifelong Illness*, 43 NATION'S HEALTH 9 (2013). In *Bearder v. State*, 806 N.W.2d 766 (Minn. 2011), parents of 25 children sued the Minnesota Department of Health and its Commissioner for "collecting, using, storing, and disseminating the children's blood samples and test results without obtaining written informed consent in violation of the Genetic Privacy Act." *Id.* at 766. To the extent that Minnesota authorities used blood samples for unrelated research, the court held that they exceeded their authority under the state's screening statutes. *Id.* at 776.

Government requirements that persons be tested or screened without consent for public health purposes can implicate 4th Amendment prohibitions of "unreasonable searches and seizures." The U.S. Supreme Court has clarified that the 4th Amendment applies to physical searches of one's person, effects, or property as well as bodily searches (e.g., blood or DNA tests). *See Skinner v. Railway Labor Execs. Ass'n,* 489 U.S. 602 (1989) (alcohol and drug testing of railway employees is reasonable and consistent with need for public safety); *Maryland v. King*, 133 S. Ct. 1 (2013) (DNA testing of arrestees via cheek swabs presents only a minimal intrusion on defendants' expectation of privacy).

Under the 4th Amendment government must generally issue a warrant based on probable cause prior to initiating a search. *Contra In re Application of the U.S.A. for Historical Cell Site Data*, No. 11–20884, 2013 WL 3914484 (5th Cir. July 30, 2013) (allowing the warrantless search of cellular device location records for law enforcement purposes). Through the "special needs doctrine," government may conduct searches without a warrant (outside the context of law enforcement) when requiring one would be impractical or impossible. *See also* discussion of searches of premises in Chapter 9.

In *Ferguson v. City of Charleston*, 532 U.S. 67 (2001), a local policy requiring the non-consensual testing of pregnant women or new mothers for drug-related conditions (notably cocaine) at a state-run university hospital in South Carolina was challenged as an unlawful search. Initially implemented in the 1990s during what some called an epidemic of "crack babies," the public health purpose underlying the screening program was to identify women who exposed their fetuses or infants to illicit drugs through maternal-child transmission. Test results were also reported to local law enforcement for potential prosecution of the mothers. The end result was pernicious, noted the Supreme Court, in linking unsuspecting, often African-American women seeking publicly-funded maternal care with criminal charges. The testing policy did not comport with the special needs doctrine, and was thus declared unconstitutional. *Id.* at 84. *See also Glover v. Eastern Neb. Cmty. Office of Retardation*, 867 F.2d 461 (8th Cir. 1989) (public agency employees serving mentally disabled persons cannot be required to be tested for Hepatitis

B and HIV where the risk to patients was insufficient to justify the intrusion on privacy).

C. TREATMENT & RELATED THERAPIES

One of the primary benefits of public health testing and screening programs involving humans is the potential to match positive cases with available treatments. Treatment services are provided often through private sector health practitioners, although many states continue to fund government-run public health clinics that deliver basic health services often to the most needy in the community. Funding crises threaten the future existence of public health clinics in some jurisdictions. *See, e.g.,* Bobby Kerlik, *Pennsylvania Supreme Court Halts Corbett Plan to Close Health Centers,* PITTSBURGH TRIB.-REV., July 18, 2013 (temporary injunction of Governor's plan to shut down 26 of the state's public health centers).

When effective treatments exist, failing to make them available for persons who are tested or screened via public health programs is unethical. STEPHEN HOLLAND, PUBLIC HEALTH ETHICS 162 (2007). Otherwise, there are few legal hurdles to implementing voluntary treatment programs so long as options are explained to individuals and they are given meaningful opportunities for informed consent. *See Canterbury v. Spence*, 464 F.2d 772 (D.C. Cir. 1972). Legal issues related to consent concerning treatment of minors may arise. In *Anspach ex rel. Anspach v. City of Phila.*, 503 F.3d 256 (3rd Cir. 2007), parents objected to the provision of contraceptives to their 16–year-old daughter at a local public health clinic. The court rejected their claim that the clinic's services were coercive and contrary to their constitutional parental rights because the court deemed the services as voluntary in nature.

Significant constitutional questions come up when treatment for communicable diseases is no longer optional either because government sets significant conditions for its receipt (e.g., release from isolation) or forces a person to be treated. Concerning conditional treatment, public health powers are sufficiently broad to require individuals to complete treatment as a condition of participation in specific activities or release from confinement where:

- Absent treatment, the individual's communicable condition and behaviors present health risks to others;

- Treatment options do not place the individual at greater risk of harm;

- Requirements for completion of treatment are reasonable, appropriate, and consistent with the current standard of care; and

- Adequate procedural due process protections are followed (as discussed in Chapter 3).

1.   DIRECTLY-OBSERVED THERAPY

One prominent example of conditional treatment predominately used in treating persons with TB (and potentially other communicable diseases requiring long treatment regimens) is directly-observed therapy (DOT). DOT is designed to assure an infected individual is fully treated by requiring a public health worker, health care practitioner, or a family member to administer or observe the individual receiving regular treatments (e.g., ingesting pills or receiving injections). DOT has proven efficacious in assuring execution of TB treatment, limiting the development of drug resistant strains of TB (which may stem from incompletions of drug regimens), and lowering the potential for further transmission. It is legally authorized in many states (*see, e.g.*, N.M. STAT. ANN. § 24–1–15.1 (2009)), particularly for persons with TB who voluntarily comply, and sometimes applied mandatorily for recalcitrant patients (*see City of Newark v. J.S.*, 652 A.2d 265 (N.J. Super. 1993); *City of Milwaukee v. Washington*, 735 N.W.2d 111 (Wis. 2007)), or prisoners (*see De Gidio v. Pung*, 704 F. Supp. 922 (D. Minn. 1989)).

2. EXPEDITED PARTNER THERAPY

Another type of conditional treatment is known as expedited partner therapy (EPT). CDC first issued a national recommendation for its use in 2006. CDC, *STD Treatment Guidelines,* 55 MMWR 5, 5–6 (Aug. 4, 2006). The public health concept underlying EPT is straight-forward: when treating patients with STIs like Chlamydia or gonorrhea, sufficient doses of prescribed antibiotics should be provided for the patients and their close sexual partners. Providing treatment for both the patient and partner reduces reinfections and the spread of STIs by breaking the circle of transmission.

Legal dilemmas related to EPT concern the provision or dispensing of a drug to the partner who has not been diagnosed by a health care practitioner or received a prescription in the normal course of health or pharmaceutical care. The potential for adverse events for the partner, misuse of the antibiotic leading to drug resistance, and liability for issuing prescriptions without examining an individual all pose potential legal obstacles to its practice across states. James G. Hodge, Jr. et al., *EPT: Assessing the Legal Environment,* 98 AM. J. PUB. HEALTH 23, 23–28 (2008).

Multiple states have overcome these arguments through direct legislative or regulatory authorization for EPT. In some jurisdictions, legal allowance of EPT is incorporated by reference to existing CDC guidance. In other places, purported legal concerns may not actually prohibit its practice. An extensive assessment of state public health laws in 2008 under the auspices of the CDC found that most states' laws already support, or at least do not prevent, EPT in practice. *Id.* Continued legislative and regulatory reforms in remaining jurisdictions have helped further its practice to a point where it is permissible or potentially allowable in 44 states. CDC, *Legal Status of Expedited Partner Therapy: EPT* (Apr. 23, 2013).

3.   FORCED TREATMENT

Courts are highly reticent to allow the confinement of autonomous individuals for the purpose of administering forced treatment or medication (notwithstanding potential exercises of DOT discussed above). The Supreme Court has espoused that individual liberty interests via substantive due process include rights to refuse treatment and sustenance. *See Cruzan v. Director, Mo. Dep't of Health*, 497 U.S. 261 (1990). Whether the Court would counter-balance this interest with a compelling public health need to allow forcible treatment of autonomous adults is uncertain. In one case, a local homeless woman with TB who failed to adhere to DOT was placed in a county jail because she posed a threat to the public's health. The Wisconsin Supreme Court upheld her confinement because the jail was "a place where proper care and treatment [would] be provided [and] the spread of disease [would] be prevented," with no less restrictive means available. *In re Washington*, 735 N.W.2d 111, 114 (Wis. 2007); *see also City of New York v. Antoinette*, 630 N.Y.S.2d 1008 (S. Queens Cty. 1995) (allowing forcible detention of person with active TB in hospital based on clear and convincing evidence that detention was necessary).

The U.S. Supreme Court has clarified that compelled medication of prisoners or other wards related to communicable diseases is permissible provided it is appropriate and essential for the health or safety of the individual or others in the absence of less intrusive alternatives. *See Riggins v.*

Nevada, 504 U.S. 127 (1992). If the safety of the individual or others is not at stake, however, medication may not be forced even in relation to wards of the state. *See Sell v. U.S.*, 539 U.S. 166 (2003) (requiring stricter assessment for forced medication of prisoner with antipsychotic drugs solely to render him fit to stand trial).

D. PARTNER NOTIFICATION

Testing, screening, and treatment are essential tools to find and address "index cases," or persons that have specific communicable conditions. An additional practice often coupled with these interventions, especially with conditions like HIV/AIDS, TB, or bioterrorism agents, is traditionally known as "contact tracing," and modernly as "partner notification" or "partner counseling and referral services" (PCRS).

Under any of these titles, the basic premise is to seek the assistance of an infected person to help locate and notify contacts or partners of their potential exposure. Partner notification generally entails infected individuals working with their health providers or public health officials to identify prospective partners. For example, following confirmation of a positive HIV test, a doctor or practitioner at a local public health clinic may ask an individual if she has had any unprotected sexual contact with others recently. Based on this information, she may be encouraged to (1) notify her partners of their potential exposure, (2) seek the doctor's assistance in notifying them, or (3) permit the local public health department to provide this information.

In the latter 2 instances, notification of the partners is combined typically with testing, counseling, and treatment referrals. In each case, notice is intended to be non-identifiable (i.e., a practitioner does not directly identify the index case who exposed a partner to HIV). In reality, some partners can identify the source of their exposure. For example, a person who is in a long-term monogamous sexual relationship may easily know who exposed her to HIV. Although unintended, the potential for identification of index cases under these forms of partner notification raises significant health information privacy issues (discussed further in Chapter 7). As well, sometimes an index case may face physical or mental abuse from notified partners. Richard L. North & Karen H. Rothenberg, *Partner Notification and the Threat of Domestic Violence Against Women with HIV Infection,* 329 NEW ENG. J. MED. 1194 (1993).

When conducted via government, PCRS participation may also implicate rights against self-incrimination protected via the 5th Amendment. A local public health official may ask an adult with HIV to identify potential sexual contacts who may include minors. The adult's participation in unprotected sexual acts with a minor may be criminal under multiple state laws in several jurisdictions. *See* Zita Lazzarini et al., *Criminalization of HIV Transmission and Exposure: Research and Policy Agenda,* 103 AM. J. PUB.

HEALTH 1350 (2013); *People v. Dempsey*, 610 N.E.2d 208 (Ill. Ct. App. 1993) (HIV+ man convicted of criminal transmission and aggravated sexual assault when he forced his 9–year old brother to perform oral sex on him); THOMAS SHEVORY, NOTORIOUS H.I.V.: THE MEDIA SPECTACLE OF NUSHAWN WILLIAMS (2004) (documenting prosecution of Williams for allegedly having unprotected sex with multiple minors after having received HIV+ test result). On May 23, 2013, it was reported that Williams may never have been HIV+. *See* Jay Tokasz, *Nushawn Williams Jury to Hear Results of His HIV Testing by Electron Microscope*, BUFFALO NEWS, June 12, 2013.

For these reasons, partner notification practices almost always involve the voluntary assent of the index case, except in rare instances. However, access to specific information about others' exposure might be deemed essential to thwart major threats to the public's health such as an outbreak of smallpox caused by bioterrorists.

E. VACCINATION

Widespread vaccination of the population is one of the premier public health achievements of the 20th century due in part to legal support at all levels of government. The federal Food and Drug Administration (FDA) is authorized to approve vaccines for use in the population. CDC's Advisory Committee on Immunization Practices (ACIP) annually sets vaccination requirements and recommendations, which most states follow in part as a condition of the receipt of federal vaccine funds. DHHS uses these recommendations and other data to provide incentives for the manufacture of vaccines and set expectations for public or private insurance coverage. Steven H. Woolf & Doug Campos-Outcalt, *Severing the Link Between Coverage Policy and the USPSTF*, 309 JAMA 1899 (2013).

All states require vaccination of children and adolescents for a host of communicable diseases as a condition of attendance at elementary, secondary, and occasionally higher education schools. Local and state departments of education and health collaborate to monitor the administration of school vaccination requirements. Increasingly states also tie attendance at day-care or other operations to completion of vaccination regimens. *See* CDC, SCHOOL AND CHILDCARE VACCINATION SURVEYS 1 (2007–2008).

Public health authorities routinely operate vaccine information campaigns and drives in response to annual influenza, help set policies for vaccinating health care workers in the public and private sectors, and encourage or require vaccination in real-time during outbreaks or emergency events. In most cases, vaccines are administered with consent of the individual or a minor's parent or guardian, although the scope of consent varies. In *Boyd v. Louisiana Med. Mut. Ins. Co.*, 593 So. 2d 427 (La. Ct. App. 1991), the court held that informed consent did not have to include notice of the 1 in 8 million risk of contracting polio from a vaccine because a reasonable person with knowledge of this risk would still take it.

The Supreme Court approved government's imposition of vaccines to control epidemic diseases in 1905 in *Jacobson* (discussed in Chapter 3), and separately endorsed school vaccination programs in 1922. *Zucht v. King*, 260 U.S. 174 (1922). Still, vaccination implementation across jurisdictions is inconsistent in part because of legal exceptions. Based on respect of 1st Amendment freedom of religion principles (discussed in Chapter 3), nearly all states (except Mississippi and West Virginia) allow for religious exemptions from school vaccination requirements. More than 20 states also recognize philosophically-based exceptions. Saad B. Omer et al., *Vaccination Policies and Rates of Exemption from Immunizations: 2005–2011*, 367 NEW ENG. J. MED. 1170 (Sept. 2012).

Standards for administering these exceptions vary across jurisdictions. In some states, parents seeking exemptions for their children must (1) provide significant, notarized documentation of their sincere religious beliefs and proof of their denomination's rejection of vaccine; (2) participate in an education session on childhood vaccines; or (3) seek state health department or court approval. In many states, however, receiving an exception to vaccination mandates is as easy as completing and filing a form through school administration.

In an era where misinformation widely circulated through social media leads some parents to believe childhood vaccinations are the cause of autism or other childhood conditions, lax requirements for religious or philosophical exemptions can lower vaccination compliance rates in some jurisdictions. Resulting outbreaks of preventable conditions, such as measles and whooping cough, among unvaccinated children across the U.S. have increasingly become routine. Fuyuen Y. Yip et al. *Measles Outbreak Epidemiology in the U.S.*, 1993–2001, 189 J. INFECTIOUS DISEASES S54, S59 (2004).

While most state or federal courts approve statutory vaccination exceptions, constitutional conundrums under the 1st and 14th Amendments leads to divergent decisions. In *Brown v. Stone*, 378 So. 2d 218 (Miss. 1979), the Mississippi Supreme Court invalidated the state's religious exemption on equal protection grounds because most parents would not qualify for it. In *Boone v. Boozman*, 217 F. Supp. 2d 938 (E.D. Ark. 2002), a federal district court demonstrated how the companion portions of the 1st Amendment to protect religious freedom can be interpreted inappositely. It struck down Arkansas' religious-belief exemption as a violation of the Establishment Clause (because it had the purpose or effect of advancing religion) as well as the Free Exercise Clause (because it supported the religious rights of those within a "recognized church or religious denomination" but not others). To override the court's decision, the Arkansas legislature subsequently reformed the exceptions language in the statute. ARK. CODE ANN. § 6–18–702(d) (2005) (vaccination is not required "if the parents or legal guardian[s] of [a] child object thereto on the grounds that immunization conflicts with [their] religious or philosophical beliefs." *Id.* at § 6–18–702(d)(4)(A)).

Both of these cases differ from most courts' permissive view of the constitutionality of religious or philosophical vaccine exemptions. Yet, they reflect the considerable legal tensions at stake in the implementation of vaccines against the backdrop of religious beliefs and public misperceptions about vaccines' risks. *See, e.g.,* James G. Hodge, Jr. & Lawrence O. Gostin, *School Vaccination Requirements: Historical, Social, and Legal Perspectives,* 90 Ky. L.J. 831 (2002).

When negative outcomes related to the administration of vaccines occur, the National Vaccine Injury Compensation Program, created in 1986, provides no-fault relief for affected persons provided they can show their injuries or deaths are related to the administration of a vaccine listed by the Program. National Childhood Vaccine Injury Act of 1986, 42 U.S.C. §§ 300aa-1 to 300aa-34 (2012). To date, nearly 15,000 claims have been adjudicated through appointed Special Masters. HEALTH RES. SERVS. ADMIN., NATIONAL VACCINE INJURY COMPENSATION PROGRAM, STATISTIC REPORTS: ADJUDICATIONS (June 26, 2013). Primary recourse through the Program is necessitated in part by the Act's limitation on state-based claims for damages related to design defects (discussed in Chapter 6) of vaccines. *See Brusewitz v. Wyeth,* 131 S. Ct. 1068 (2011). Additional vaccine-related liability protections stemming from preparedness and response efforts in declared emergencies are discussed in Chapter 10.

F. SOCIAL DISTANCING MEASURES

The legal powers to prevent and control communicable diseases through testing, screening, treatment, and vaccination are core facets of public health practice. Sometimes public health authorities must respond through powers designed not only to detect and deter infectious diseases, but also to separate individuals and populations who pose risks to others. Through social distancing measures, public health agents create space among individuals and groups to thwart the spread of communicable conditions.

Quarantine, isolation, curfew, and closure are among the oldest public health powers. Although wielded historically in ways that occasionally castigated affected persons, the purpose of these measures is not punitive. Rather, they are designed solely to limit the spread of air-borne or other easily-transmitted conditions, particularly when other interventions are ineffective. Still, application and enforcement of these measures can affect constitutional rights to freedom of movement, bodily integrity, and privacy. For these reasons, social distancing techniques may be administered or enforced sparingly despite sometimes broad legal authorization at the state or local levels.

While all social distancing measures share the same basic goal of separating healthy and infectious individuals to limit further transmission, these powers are distinct. *Isolation* refers to the separation of a person or group of persons known or suspected to be infected with a communicable disease to prevent the spread of infection. *Quarantine* refers to the separation of a person or group presumed or known to have been exposed to a communicable disease to obviate infections with those not exposed. Simply stated, isolation involves separating infected persons while quarantine is used to separate persons merely exposed to infectious conditions. All states' public health laws authorize the isolation or quarantine of individuals related to varied communicable diseases. TFAH, READY OR NOT? PROTECTING THE PUBLIC'S HEALTH IN THE AGE OF BIOTERRORISM (2004).

CDC possesses its own limited federal power to quarantine or isolate individuals with specific infectious diseases, as well as operate several quarantine stations in major transportation hubs across the U.S. James J. Misrahi et al., *HHS/CDC Legal Response to SARS Outbreak*, 10 EMERGING INFECTIOUS DISEASES 353 (2004). Its powers to quarantine were tested in a well-publicized case in 2007. Andrew Speaker, an attorney practicing in Atlanta (CDC's home base), contracted TB during prior travels. Although local health authorities in Georgia asked him to limit his future travel, Speaker left Atlanta's airport for an extensive European trip. While away, CDC determined that he may have developed XDR-TB. They notified Speaker and asked him to report to health authorities in Italy where he was located at the time. He refused. Following an international media storm, Speaker eventually returned to the U.S. days later by flying into Canada and driving across the border into New York State.

Upon his return, CDC issued its 1st federal quarantine order since 1963. Speaker surrendered to public health authorities and received treatment at a Denver hospital that regularly treats TB patients. Multiple persons close to Speaker during his extensive travel were briefly placed under limited quarantine to ascertain whether they had contracted TB. Eventually CDC determined that Speaker never had XDR-TB, but instead a more common and less severe type of the disease. A subsequent lawsuit brought by Speaker against CDC alleging privacy and other violations was summarily dismissed on September 14, 2012. *Speaker v. CDC*, 489 F. App'x 425 (11th Cir. 2012). Events surrouding this example reveal the difficulties of implementing modern quarantine orders as well as the complex balance of public and private interests at stake. *See* David P. Fidler et al., *Through the Quarantine Looking Glass: Drug-Resistant TB and Public Health Governance, Law and Ethics,* 35 J.L. MED. & ETHICS 526, 526–33 (2007).

Curfews and *closures* are typically used in response to epidemics, mass disasters, or following particular outbreaks of food-borne illnesses from commercial or other sources. They are designed to set limits on the time or place regarding the assembly of individuals so as to mitigate the spread of disease. State or local public health officers may, for example, issue orders to set curfew for communities affected by disease to disassociate individuals temporarily from gathering in large groups. Provided orders for curfews are necessary, temporary infringements on individuals' liberty, notably their right to travel, are allowed. *See In re Juan C.*, 33 Cal. Rptr. 2d 919, 922 (Cal. Ct. App. 1994) ("Though the right to travel ... is constitutionally protected, [it] may be legitimately curtailed [via curfew] when a community has been ravaged by flood, fire or disease, and its safety and welfare are threatened." (citing *Zemel v. Rusk,* 381 U.S. 1, 15–16 (1965)). Closure orders may be implemented by public health agencies (in concert with law enforcement) to shut down places that either are the source of an outbreak (e.g., a restaurant responsible for serving contaminated food) or through which disease may be spread (e.g., a school where student gatherings may further spread influenza).

Intrusions on personal liberties of these or other social distancing measures vary. Isolation or quarantine orders, for example, can significantly restrict individual movement by authorizing the forcible removal of persons from their homes for the duration of their infectivity. In reality, these orders typically seek voluntary compliance. Public health officials encourage affected individuals to remain at home and utilize universal precautions to prevent the spread of disease, unless they need particular medical care for which placement in a health care setting is more appropriate.

To support uses of coercive public health powers against judicial challenges, public health authorities must be prepared to show that:

- The subject of social distancing measures is actually, or is reasonably suspected of, being infectious or exposed to infectious conditions;

- The subject poses a specific threat to the public's health. For example, quarantine of a group of persons concerning their exposure to an infectious condition, such as smallpox, is warranted to prevent the transmission of a deadly pathogen spread via bioterrorism. Quarantine of a group of persons exposed to annual influenza, which does not substantially threaten most persons' health, is likely unlawful;

- The terms of placement are safe and habitable. In 1900, the South Carolina Supreme Court struck down a quarantine order served on an older woman with leprosy in part because she was removed from her "cottage" home to a "pesthouse, coarse and comfortless." *Kirk v. Wyman*, 65 S.E. 387 (S.C. 1909);

- The terms of confinement are warranted. In 1892, about 1,200 Russian Jews were quarantined unjustifiably in 1892 outside New York City. Most (about 1,150) were healthy people who unfortunately lived in proximity to 50 ship passengers who had developed typhus. HOWARD MARKEL, QUARANTINE! 59 (1997). In *Jew Ho v. Williamson*, 103 F. 10 (N.D. Cal. 1900), a federal district court outlawed a plague-related quarantine order over several blocks of modern-day Chinatown in San Francisco as "unreasonable, unjust, . . . oppressive," and discriminatory. *Id.* at 26; and

- Procedural due process is provided (as noted in Chapter 3). In *Greene v. Edwards*, 263 S.E.2d 661 (W. Va. 1980), the West Virginia Supreme Court required public health authorities to apply the same procedural protections concerning the involuntary commitment of persons with mental illness to those confined because of their infection with TB. This includes an adequate notice, right to a hearing, right to counsel, right to present and confront witnesses, right to a verbatim transcript, and implementation of a clear and convincing standard to warrant isolation. *Id.* at 663.

In summary, modern courts tend to strictly scrutinize impositions of social distancing measures that affect individual liberties and bodily privacy. Public health authorities must demonstrate a compelling governmental interest in support of a well-targeted intervention for which there is no less restrictive alternative. LAWRENCE O. GOSTIN, PUBLIC HEALTH LAW: POWER, DUTY, RESTRAINT 444–45 (2d ed. 2008). Even as courts continue to defer to the judgments of legislators or regulators as to the need for specific public health interventions (consistent with separation of powers), constitutional requirements can limit the use of significant public health powers to control infectious diseases.

Communicable diseases will always be a primary part of the public health agenda, but additional legal challenges arise from the emergence of chronic conditions. Collectively, these conditions comprise major new foci for public health improvement. Some traditional legal powers, such as testing and screening, are aptly applied to non-communicable conditions. Other powers, like quarantine and isolation, have little use related to chronic conditions. As a result, new legal routes to counter varying threats to community health must be considered. Exploration of these paths begins in Chapter 5.

CHAPTER 5

ADDRESSING CHRONIC CONDITIONS

While communicable diseases discussed in Chapter 4 comprise considerable public health efforts, greater impacts on population health in the 21st century have emanated from chronic conditions. Sensational diseases like avian flu or HIV/AIDS grab the public's attention as to how public health authorities intervene, but heart disease, cancers, diabetes, and other conditions are the real killers across society. Though defying precise definition, chronic conditions are at the source of millions of deaths in the U.S. and contribute to massive disability among the living. Though caused by multiple factors, chronic conditions share a common facet: they are often preventable. How law can be a tool in the fight against avoidable morbidity and mortality stemming from chronic illnesses requires a close examination of the scope and limits of public health efforts to alter individual and population-based behaviors.

A. CHRONIC CONDITIONS—DEFINED

Unlike communicable conditions, most chronic conditions are not transferred directly between humans or from other vectors to humans. Beyond this, defining chronic conditions is subject to interpretation. Richard A. Goodman et al., *Defining and Measuring Chronic Conditions: Imperatives for*

Research, Policy, Program, and Practice, 10 PREVENTING CHRONIC DISEASE E66 (2013).

Physicians, researchers, epidemiologists, and law- and policy-makers disagree over a precise definition. Chronic conditions are generally characterized by their "uncertain etiology, multiple risk factors, . . . long latency period, . . . prolonged course of illness, noncontagious origin, functional impairment or disability, and incurability." Matthew McKenna & Janet L. Collins, *Current Issues and Challenges in Chronic Disease Control, in* PATRICK L. REMINGTON ET AL., CHRONIC DISEASE EPIDEMIOLOGY AND CONTROL 1–24 (2d ed. 2010). These characterizations, however, hardly clarify what is and is not included.

DHHS defines chronic illnesses as those "conditions that last a year or more and require ongoing medical attention and/or limit activities of daily living." DHHS, MULTIPLE CHRONIC CONDITIONS: A STRATEGIC FRAMEWORK 2 (2010). Under this conception, chronic conditions thus include heart disease, many cancers, diabetes, and clinical depression, but not the common cold, broken bones, or pregnancy.

No matter how defined, the health care costs and public health impacts of physical or mental chronic conditions on disability, morbidity, and mortality in the U.S. are staggering. Chronic illnesses are the nation's leading contributor to death and disability. According to CDC, 70% of all deaths each year are attributable to chronic conditions; 50% of all adults have at least 1 such condition (and nearly ½ of them have multiple conditions); and 26% of the American population is limited in their daily activities by these conditions. Nearly 75% of health care costs annually are devoted to their treatment. CDC, CHRONIC DISEASES AND HEALTH PROMOTION (2013). Worse yet, "[t]he number and proportion of Americans living with chronic conditions [are] increasing" as the population ages. By 2030 it is predicted that over 170 million Americans will have multiple chronic conditions. GERARD ANDERSON, CHRONIC CARE: MAKING THE CASE FOR ONGOING CARE 9 (2010).

While the types and impacts of chronic conditions vary by population (e.g., children, adults, elderly), major examples include:

- *Heart disease*—Nearly ¼ of U.S. deaths annually (600,000) are caused by heart disease. Kenneth D. Kochanek et al., *Deaths: Final Data for 2009*, 60 NAT'L VITAL STAT. REP. 3 (2011). Costs of health care services, medications, and lost productivity related to coronary heart disease alone exceeded $108 billion in 2011. Paul A. Heidenreich et al., *Forecasting the Future of Cardiovascular Disease in the U.S.*, 123 CIRCULATION 933 (2011).

- *Cancers*—Even as the definition of cancer is changing, its collective impact on human health is incredible. *See* Tara Parker-Pope, *Scientists Urge Narrower Rules to Define Cancer*, N.Y. TIMES, July 30, 2013, at A1. In 2013, over 1.66 million new cases of cancer arose, with projected deaths of 580,350 in the U.S., many by lung cancers caused by smoking (228,190). Rebecca Siegel et al., *Cancer Statistics 2013*, 63 CA: CANCER J. FOR CLINICIANS 1, 11–30 (2013).

- *Diabetes*—Type 1 and 2 diabetes affect 25.8 million people (8.3% of the U.S. population). Nearly 2 million people age 20 years or over were newly diagnosed with diabetes in 2010. It is the leading cause of kidney failure, non-traumatic lower limb amputations, and new cases of blindness among adults. CDC, NATIONAL DIABETES FACT SHEET 8 (2011).

Additional chronic conditions with catastrophic effects on the population's health include Alzheimer's disease, arthritis, asthma, chronic obstructive pulmonary disease (COPD), depression, epilepsy, glaucoma, hemophilia, hypertension, osteoporosis, post-traumatic stress disorder (PTSD), and stroke.

B. CAUSES OF CHRONIC CONDITIONS

The causes of chronic conditions are as diverse as the conditions themselves. Contributing factors include genetics, stress, occupation, socioeconomic status, environmental exposures, adverse medical events, and lack of access to public health or health care services.

Dietary factors are also at play in relation to the proliferation of these conditions. Three of the 4 primary modifiable health risk behaviors at the source of most chronic conditions relate to what Americans consume. These 3 behaviors are poor nutrition, tobacco use, and excessive alcohol consumption (physical inactivity is the 4th). Regular ingestion and use of "consumable vices," including tobacco, alcohol, sugar, salt, and high-fat foods, contribute significantly to the development of chronic diseases. *See* DAVID A. KESSLER, THE END OF OVEREATING: TAKING CONTROL OF THE INSATIABLE AMERICAN APPETITE (2009).

CDC suggests that poor dietary choices coupled with low levels of physical activity are the leading causes of death annually in the U.S. This finding comports with major increases in rates of obesity among children, adolescents, and adults over the past 3 decades. When CDC first began to measure national obesity rates in 1966, approximately 13% of adults were considered obese and 4% of kids were considered overweight. By 2010, using similar criteria, nearly 36% of American adults are obese, and 33% of children and adolescents are obese or overweight. James G. Hodge, Jr. et al., *New Frontiers in Obesity Control: Innovative Public Health Legal Interventions,* 5 DUKE FORUM FOR L. & SOC. CHANGE 1 (2013).

Absent changes, the future of Americans' battle with obesity is bleak. The Trust for America's Health (TFAH) projected in 2012 that adult obesity rates would climb to 44% by 2030, costing up to $66 billion in direct health care costs and $580 billion in lost economic productivity per year. TFAH, F AS IN FAT: HOW OBESITY THREATENS AMERICA'S FUTURE

28 (2012). Only recently have public health officials recognized small declines in obesity rates. In August 2013, CDC reported that obesity rates among preschool-age children from poor families fell based on 2008–2011 data from nearly 20 jurisdictions — "the first time a major government report has shown a consistent pattern of decline for low-income children after decades of rising rates." Sabrina Tavernise, *Poor Children Show a Decline in Obesity Rate,* N.Y. TIMES, Aug. 7, 2013, at A1.

Tobacco products used regularly by nearly 20% of Americans are a major contributing factor to over 440,000 annual deaths in the U.S. CDC, *Smoking-Attributable Mortality, Years of Potential Life Lost, and Productivity Losses—U.S., 2000—2004,* 57 MMWR 1226 (Nov. 14, 2008). Excessive alcohol consumption contributes to over 50 different diseases and injuries that in sum constitute the 3rd leading preventable cause of death. CDC, ALCOHOL USE AND HEALTH (2013). Many Americans' high salt diets raise substantially the risk of coronary heart disease, stroke, heart attack, and kidney damage. Theodore A. Kotchen, *Salt in Health and Disease—a Delicate Balance,* 368 NEW ENG. J. MED. 1229 (2013).

Recent studies concerning the impacts of over-consumption of sugar in American's diets led an observer to conclude that "[s]ugar is indeed toxic." Mark Bittman, Editorial, *It's The Sugar, Folks,* N.Y. TIMES, Feb. 28, 2013, at A23. One study links ingestion of sugar, largely through beverages, to 25,000 deaths in the U.S. in 2010 (and 180,000 deaths globally). Gitanjali M. Singh et al., *Mortality Due to SSB Consumption: A Global, Regional, and National Comparative Risk Assessment,* 127 CIRCULATION AMP22 (2013). In another global study, researchers conclusively link increased ingestion of sugar with higher rates of diabetes, independent of rates of obesity. Sanjay Basu et al., *The Relationship of Sugar to Population-Level Diabetes Prevalence: An Econometric Analysis of Repeated Cross-Sectional Data*, 8 PLoS ONE e57873 (2013).

C. LEGAL AUTHORITIES CONCERNING CHRONIC CONDITIONS

Chronic conditions differ from communicable ones in many ways, but similar public health powers can be used to address their incidence. *See, e.g.,* Wendy C. Perdue et al., *A Legal Framework for Preventing Cardiovascular Disease*, 29 AM. J. PREVENTIVE MED. 139 (2005). Public health laws authorizing counseling, testing, screening, and treatment are used extensively to counteract chronic conditions. Federal and state recommendations for testing and screening of various cancers, often based on guidance from medical and public health organizations, are routinely followed by health care practitioners. Even vaccinations may help stymie the rate of some chronic conditions. To the extent that HPV vaccine deters infection, individuals can avoid the onset of related cancers of the reproductive organs and other parts of the body. As a result, CDC recommends HPV vaccines for boys and girls beginning at ages 11–12. CDC,

Recommendations on the Use of Quadrivalent HPV in Males—ACIP, 2011, 60 MMWR 1705, 1707 (Dec. 23, 2011). Though safe and efficacious, uptake of HPV vaccinations nationally has been curtailed by political and other views focused on limiting access to a vaccine to prevent STIs to adolescents prior to an acceptable age. *See* James Colgrove et al., *HPV Vaccination Mandates—Lawmaking amid Political and Scientific Controversy*, 363 NEW ENG. J. MED. 785, 787 (2010); CDC, *HPV Coverage Among Adolescent Girls, 2007–2012, and Postlicensure Vaccine Safety Monitoring, 2006–2013–U.S.*, 62 MMWR 591, 594 (July 26, 2013).

Education campaigns alert the public to risks (sometimes through graphic illustrations) of chronic conditions related to tobacco, alcohol, or drug use. A New York City health department education campaign in 2009 targeted the ingestion of sugar-sweetened beverages (SSBs) through advertisements depicting consumers gulping down thick globs of fat. Sewell Chan, *New Targets in the Fat Fight: Soda and Juice*, N.Y. TIMES, Sept. 1, 2009, at A22. Additional discussion of public health education is provided in Chapter 8.

Not all public health powers used to prevent communicable diseases apply to chronic conditions. Social distancing measures often lack utility (and constitutionality) when applied to most chronic conditions. Other public health powers are thus needed to: (1) alter individual and group behaviors contributing to the onset of chronic illness; (2) change environmental impacts that lend to their proliferation; or (3) prevent factors in which such illnesses may arise or result in significant harms to individuals or the public. Core among these legal strategies are the powers to tax and spend; regulatory laws directly governing the environment and private sector; and anti-discrimination protections. Each of these legal areas is discussed below.

1. THE POWER TO TAX

Governments' powers to tax involve more than raising revenue. These powers are used strategically and lawfully to change or alter behaviors, often in the interests of preventing or treating chronic conditions. The power to tax necessarily includes the power to spend, including setting significant conditions on how governmental resources may be used when doled out to public or private entities (discussed below). At its core, governments' "power over the purse" allows it considerable discretion in collecting and disbursing individual and corporate resources for the betterment of society. ERWIN CHEMERINSKY, CONSTITUTIONAL LAW: PRINCIPLES AND POLICIES 279–80 (4th ed. 2011).

While each level of government has some authority to tax, the federal government's taxing prowess (pursuant to U.S. CONST. art. I, § 8) is considerable. Particularly since the institution of national income taxes in 1913, Congress has used its taxing authority extensively. ROY G. BLAKEY & GLADYS C. BLAKEY, THE FEDERAL INCOME TAX 71 (2006). As Chief Justice Roberts noted in 2012 in the Supreme Court's decision on the constitutionality of the ACA, the power to tax includes the power to "affect individual conduct." *National Fed. of Ind. Bus. v. Sebelius,* 132 S. Ct. 2566, 2596 (2012).

So long as it acts consistent with principles of federalism and individual rights, Congress can (and does) use its taxing power in the interests of the public's health. Related to the prevention and control of chronic illnesses, for example, the federal government (and many states) tax products like tobacco to help discourage their consumption. DHSS & CDC, REDUCING TOBACCO USE: A REPORT OF THE SURGEON GENERAL 337 (2000). They do so based on the proven economic theory that to the extent taxes substantially raise the price of cigarettes, people will smoke less, and their overall health and risk of developing chronic conditions will improve. *Id.* at 359. On this same basis, some states and localities have considered taxing junk foods or high-calorie beverages to limit consumption. Michael F. Jacobson & Kelly D. Brownell, *Small Taxes on Soft Drinks and Snack Foods to Promote Health,* 90 AM. J. PUB. HEALTH 854 (2000).

The flip-side of direct taxation to change consumer behaviors is the use of tax subsidies or credits to encourage product purchases or other market factors in the interests of the public's health. Congress, for example, created positive tax incentives for individuals to purchase individual health insurance through the ACA. By encouraging employees to obtain insurance, access to preventive and other health services may be expanded with direct public health benefits.

Raucous political debates over the passage of the ACA, and many other tax-related measures in Congress and across the states, reflect political realities in creating new tax schemes to positively change consumer behaviors. The public and its legislative representatives often disdain new taxes, especially when they are used to change behaviors of millions of Americans. Yet, when politically viable, government's use of its direct power to tax to address chronic conditions is virtually without limit.

2.   THE POWER TO SPEND

Collecting revenues through taxes also allows governments to disburse resources in ways that promote the "general welfare," including communal health. And whenever government, particularly at the federal level, has money to spend, it may set conditions on its receipt. Through its constitutional powers to spend, Congress may lawfully impose a myriad of conditions on the disbursement of federal funds to which tribal, state, or local governments (or private entities) must adhere. CHEMERINSKY, CONSTITUTIONAL LAW at 285–86. Of course, any public or private entity can always reject specific conditions attached to funding streams, but they will lose access to sometimes significant public health resources.

Examples of Congress' use of its spending power to address chronic (or other) conditions are broad. They range from the setting of conditions on the receipt of basic health care resources (e.g., Medicaid) to specific allotments for public health surveillance (e.g., HIV/AIDS reporting, discussed in Chapter 7) and research on chronic conditions like obesity and Alzheimer's disease. Though Congress' power is extensive, the Supreme Court has set some limits on the use of conditional spending, particularly between federal and state governments.

In *South Dakota v. Dole*, 483 U.S. 203 (1987), the Court approved Congress' condition that states seeking select highway transportation funds upgrade their drinking age to 21 (largely to reduce alcohol-related crashes and fatalities on federal highways). Rejecting a federalism-based challenge, Chief Justice Rehnquist clarified that Congress' exercise of its conditional spending power is constitutional as applied to the states provided:

(a)   it serves some general purpose (for which the Court is typically deferential consistent with separation of powers);

(b)   the choices and conditions are clear and unambiguous;

(c)   the conditions are related to some national project or program;

(d)   states are not induced to engage in unconstitutional acts (e.g., use of federal funds to discriminate against persons on the basis of race). In *Agency for Int'l Dev. v. Alliance for Open Soc'y Int'l,* 133 S. Ct. 2321 (2013), the Court struck down an "anti-prostitution   pledge,"   which prohibited the issuance of HIV-related grants to recipients who did not affirmatively state their opposition to prostitution and sex trafficking. Such conditions violated the free speech rights of recipients under the 1st Amendment; and

(e)   states are not compelled to accept the funds. *Dole,* 483 U.S. at 207–11.

For years following *Dole,* virtually no Congressional exercise of its conditional spending power was adjudged by courts to compel states. States always have the option of rejecting federal funds if they do not like the terms. However, in the Court's decision on the constitutionality of the ACA, Congress' plan to expand the Medicaid program (providing health services to largely low-income families) to millions of newly insured was rejected. *Sebelius,* 132 S. Ct. at 2604–05.

The ACA provided each state the option of expanding its Medicaid population to include a larger proportion of low-income adults by 2014, or else face the loss of all its federal Medicaid dollars. In response to states' federalism-based challenges, Chief Justice Roberts opined that this choice represented unconstitutional compulsion on states to comply due in large part to (a) the enormous sums at stake if states chose not to expand their programs; and (b) a significant "shift in kind, not merely degree" of the original purposes of the Medicaid program via expansion. *Id.* at 2604–06. Though the Court rejected the ACA's compelled conditions, it crafted a constitutional compromise. The ACA's Medicaid deal would survive if the Centers for Medicare and Medicaid Services (CMS), part of DHHS, conditions only the states' receipt of expansion funds (instead of their entire Medicaid budget) on their willingness to extend their Medicaid populations.

In confirming greater limits on Congress' use of its spending power to set conditions for receipt of federal funds, *Sebelius* dampened Congress' ability to cover more Americans with basic health insurance, a primary public health objective of the ACA. *See, e.g.,* Nicole Huberfeld et al., *Plunging Into Endless Difficulties: Medicaid and Coercion in [NFIB v. Sebelius]*, 93 Bos. L. Rev. 1 (2013). Without the threat of losing their entire Medicaid budget, multiple states have expressed unwillingness to expand their programs (even though the federal government pays the bulk of the costs for new Medicaid enrollees over several years). Simon F. Haeder & David L. Weimer, *You Can't Make Me Do It: State Implementation of Insurance Exchanges Under the ACA*, Pub. Admin. Rev., May 2013, at 3. As a result, millions of Americans may continue to be denied access to publicly-funded, basic health services, including preventive care. The Court's decision, however, also creates new possibilities for state and local governments to challenge other federal public health spending programs, including long-standing environmental health laws, on similar grounds that the terms of receipt of federal funds are onerous and unconstitutional.

3.   THE POWER TO REGULATE

The potential to influence individual and governmental choices through the powers to tax and spend is commanding. Yet, government also has the power to regulate private entities and individuals consistent with prevention and control strategies related to chronic conditions. As noted in Chapter 3, so long as legislative bodies provide articulable standards for executive agencies to regulate, federal, tribal, state, and local public health officials can administrate and enforce laws to further the public's health.

Through public health regulation, for example, government can:

- Ban or limit the sale of products deemed harmful to the public's health (among other purposes). Following discovery of the harmful effects of lead largely on child development, its removal from paint, gasoline, and other products is now mandated;

- Limit possession of products that may harm specific populations. The federal and all state governments prohibit persons under the age of 18 from purchasing tobacco products (and some states or localities are considering raising this age to 21);

- Control how products are manufactured or sold. In some states, for example, the sale of alcohol is restricted to certain locations during set days and hours. Many states that legalize the sale of marijuana for medicinal uses set narrow manufacturing and licensing requirements to help assure the product does not find its way to unlawful purchasers or users (in violation of the federal Controlled Substances Act, 21 U.S.C. §§ 801–971 (2012));

- Require entities to create or sell products in conformity with public health mandates. As discussed in Chapter 8, the ACA, for example, requires chain restaurants across the U.S. to post calorie counts for their menu items similar to practices implemented already in several jurisdictions. With ready access to calorie data at the point of sale, consumers can make healthier choices and potentially lower their overall calorie consumption;

- Set meaningful restrictions on consumer uses of products in public places. Federal, state, and local smoke-free laws over the past several decades have targeted public environments from cars to planes to public squares to eradicate public exposures to second-hand smoke (*see, e.g.,* Amy R. Confair et al., *Factors Affecting Successful Enactment of Legislation Prohibiting Smoking in Cars with Children,* 53 JURIMETRICS J. 375 (2013)); and

- Create safer workplaces that reduce exposures to harmful elements or practices. Federal and state regulations governing coal mines have significantly reduced the incidence of "black lung" deaths. Federal workplace standards via the Occupational Safety and Health Administration (OSHA) have not only helped reduce injuries (discussed in Chapter 6), but also lowered chronic conditions among workers through workplace safety initiatives.

These notable examples are merely illustrative. Governmental regulatory powers to address chronic (and other) conditions extend into multiple facets of public and private life. Though capable of heavy-handed enforcement, public health agencies typically seek cooperative and contributive efforts among public and private actors to conceive, draft, and implement regulatory controls. In general, public health regulations are lawful so long as executive agencies act within the scope of their delegated powers, adhere to procedural requirements in creating and enforcing regulatory provisions, have legitimate public health support for the need to regulate, and do not otherwise offend constitutional or other principles of law. Particularly at the local level, complying with this latter requirement can be dubious.

In April 2011, for example, the Cleveland City Council enacted an anti-obesity ordinance to ban trans fats in foods served in restaurants and other food shops. A few months later, the Ohio legislature amended state law to prohibit municipalities from regulating the ingredients used by food servers. The net effect of the Ohio legislature's amendment of state statute was to preempt Cleveland's trans fats ordinance. The City sued the State claiming that the amendment unconstitutionally stripped the City of its home rule (discussed in Chapter 2). After the trial court decided in favor of the City, the Ohio Court of Appeals affirmed that the legislature's amendment unlawfully overrode Cleveland's home rule and, consequently, reinstated the City's trans fat ordinance. *City of Cleveland v. State*, 2013 Ohio 1186 (Ohio Ct. App. 2013).

4.   ADDRESSING DISABILITY BIAS

Many chronic conditions are by definition disabling. Persons who are impaired in their major life activities due to their chronic illness may be entitled to special protections from discrimination under the federal Americans with Disabilities Act (ADA), 42 U.S.C. §§ 12101–12213 (2012), and additional laws at the federal, state, and local levels. Implemented pursuant to Congress' interstate commerce powers, the ADA protects persons with actual disabilities as well as those who are simply regarded by others as having a disability. *Id.* at § 12102(1). Collectively, disability laws help to eliminate discrimination against some persons with chronic conditions in the workplace and many other settings.

While the dimensions of individual disability protections via the ADA are beyond the scope of this text, disability laws can contribute to the reduction of chronic illness in key ways. ADA requirements to support reasonable accommodations in many settings directly benefit persons with disabilities, but also have reciprocal benefits for others. Building redesigns (e.g., to include elevators or lifts) and retrofitting of community plans (e.g., to include ramps or paved trails) consistent with the ADA have transformed the built environment across the country, leading to safer communities that help reduce injuries and diminish chronic conditions.

Universal precautions in health care settings, ushered in part via the ADA's requirements to accommodate patients and health care workers (HCWs) with disabilities, have lowered infectious disease transmission, improved care for chronic conditions, and improved the efficiency of care in some instances. In 1 survey, over 42% of U.S. businesses report enhanced workplace safety based in part on ADA-influenced improvements. Helen A. Schartz et al., *Workplace Accommodations: Evidence Based Outcomes*, 27 WORK 345, 349 (2006). Protecting disabled workers buttresses support for indoor smoking bans to accommodate persons with asthma or other conditions, as well as improve air quality for all workers. Lainie Rutkow et al., *Banning Second-hand Smoke in Indoor Public Places Under the ADA: A Legal and Public Health Imperative*, 40 CONN. L. REV. 409, 409 (2007). Telecommuting options to assist disabled workers under the ADA help reduce commute times, lower accident rates, decrease the spread of infectious diseases, and minimize work-related stress. Brianne M. Sullenger, *Telecommuting: A Reasonable Accommodation under the ADA as Technology Advances*, 19 REGENT U. L. REV. 537, 542–43 (2006).

Disability protections addressing unwarranted discrimination, however, may be contravened by other public health laws that directly or indirectly reflect bias related to the causes of chronic conditions, or persons who suffer from them. For example, anti-tobacco policies at the federal and state levels authorize discrimination against smokers and other tobacco consumers in the interest of protecting the public's health. Smokers may not light up in many public places, can be denied life insurance outright or charged more for health insurance, or be restricted in their employment options (or not hired at all for that matter). Each of these policies have underlying legal support grounded in protecting the public's health directly or indirectly (by discouraging smoking). Yet persons with chronic illnesses, including many smokers, are largely disadvantaged.

Persons who use illicit drugs may be addicted to these substances and, consequently, greatly limited in their major life activities. However, the ADA expressly excludes illicit drug use among those items classifiable as disabilities. 42 U.S.C. § 12114 (2013). Few might agree that users of heroin, cocaine, crystal meth, or other dangerous drugs are entitled to disability rights, but policies related to their treatment are beginning to change. Once castigated and charged via criminal courts, users of addictive drugs are now provided options to avoid full prosecution so long as they participate in drug treatment programs. In Connecticut, courts are statutorily authorized to order offenders who are drug- or alcohol-dependent into treatment in lieu of prosecution or incarceration. CONN. GEN. STAT. §§ 17a-692 to 17a-701 (2013).

In June 2013, the American Medical Association (AMA) issued a national call for classifying obesity as a disease. Andrew Pollack, *A.M.A. Recognizes Obesity as a Disease,* N.Y. TIMES, June 18, 2013. If broadly adopted, this might help qualify all forms of obesity, like its associated condition, Type II diabetes, for disability protections and related health insurance coverage. Currently only "severe obesity" (when body weight is more than 100% over norm) may qualify as a disability under the ADA. EEOC COMPLIANCE MANUAL § 902.2(c)(5)(ii) (2009).

For now, obesity remains a major public health target with some policies having potentially deleterious impacts on persons who are overweight or obese. Consider proposals in some states or localities to (a) authorize charging obese persons more for their health insurance premiums (*see, e.g.,* TENN. CODE ANN. § 56–7–3013 (2013) (insurers can establish premium schedules based on obesity); or (b) set workplace wellness bonuses based on levels of physical activity (*see, e.g.,* MASS. GEN. LAWS ANN. tit. IX, ch. 62 § 6N (2013) (establishing a $10,000 tax credit for employers seeking to create a wellness program); MISS. CODE ANN. § 41–97–9 (2012) (creating model program for employee wellness including incentives).

Each of these incentive-driven policies may negatively impact persons who are overweight or obese to the extent they are charged more for similar services, cannot participate fully to garner benefits, or simply lose opportunities because of their weight. Disability protections may prevent some of these impacts (e.g., ADA employment protections apply to persons simply "regarded as" having a disability). Conversely, some public health laws and policies represent an affront to equality of persons with conditions that are, or will soon be, chronic.

––––––––––––

Addressing chronic conditions through law requires creative options and resulting trade-offs. Implementing public health laws to deter individual behaviors that lead to chronic illnesses seems overly paternalistic to some. For others, application of such laws may seem unfair related to their own conditions, the onset of which may not be of their own doing. Still, at the source of government regulatory approaches related to chronic conditions is the laudatory goal of preventing excess morbidity and mortality. Carrying out this same objective concerning injury prevention necessitates the extensive use of additional legal tools, namely civil litigation and criminal enforcement, as discussed in Chapter 6.

CHAPTER 6

MITIGATING THE INCIDENCE & SEVERITY OF INJURIES & OTHER HARMS

In addition to addressing communicable and chronic conditions, a 3rd major prong of the underlying mission of public health agencies, advocacy organizations, and other partners concerns preventing injuries and related harms or deaths. Public health practitioners define injuries broadly as "any unintentional or intentional [bodily] damage . . . resulting from acute exposure to thermal, mechanical, electrical, or chemical energy or from the absence of such essentials as heat or oxygen." NAT'L COMM. FOR INJURY PREVENTION & CONTROL, INJURY PREVENTION: MEETING THE CHALLENGE 4 (1989).

Coupled with these acute harms are long-term, chronic injuries related to repeated exposures to products like tobacco, alcohol, or drugs. Injuries arise from multiple, additional sources, some of which are unintentional (e.g., vehicle crashes) and others which are not (e.g., homicides). The collective impact of injuries on the population each year is significant, as explained in section A, below.

The public health tragedy underlying most injuries, harms, and related deaths is that they are preventable through changes in behaviors, products, and the environment via public health education (*see* Chapter 8), engineering, and the law. Many types of laws, including themes discussed already in Part 2 (e.g., screening, treatment, powers to tax and spend, regulations) are used to prevent future injuries and deaths. Two additional U.S. legal areas to prevent and control injuries and harms include tort and criminal law.

Deleterious practices leading to unintentional injuries are intrinsically tied to the role of "tort" law (or laws to address civil wrongs). Through tort litigation (or sometimes just its threat), the design, manufacture, sale, and use of an array of products including food, drugs, guns, tobacco, toys, and vehicles have changed to prevent injuries. How tort actions lead to product changes over time in the interests of consumer safety and the public's health are discussed further in section B.

Criminal law presents a different and controversial approach to addressing injuries and related deaths. By penalizing individual or corporate behaviors that contribute to injuries, the underlying public health premise of criminal law (and tort law for that matter) is that they can deter injurious acts. This premise may be limited. Take, for example, strict laws prohibiting illicit drug possession to protect individuals from harms including drug overdose deaths. Persons prosecuted under these laws may receive what some deem as just punishments, namely criminal fines and incarceration. Absent additional interventions (e.g., drug rehabilitation and treatment programs), these punishments may not only negatively impact their